SYDNEY

◉ Walking Eye App

Your Insight Guide purchase includes a free download of the destination's corresponding eBook. It is available now from the free Walking Eye container app in the App Store and Google Play. Simply download the Walking Eye container app to access the eBook dedicated to your purchased book. The app also features free information on local events taking place and activities you can enjoy during your stay, with the option to book them. In addition, premium content for a wide range of other destinations is available to purchase in-app.

HOW TO DOWNLOAD THE WALKING EYE APP

Available on purchase of this guide only.

1. Visit our website: www.insightguides.com/walkingeye
2. Download the Walking Eye container app to your smartphone (this will give you access to your free eBook and the ability to purchase other products)
3. Select the scanning module in the Walking Eye container app
4. Scan the QR Code on this page – you will be asked to enter a verification word from the book as proof of purchase
5. Download your free eBook* for travel information on the go

* Other destination apps and eBooks are available for purchase separately or are free with the purchase of the Insight Guide book

CONTENTS

ARCHITECTURE

From the rugged sandstone of the city's oldest buildings (route 1), to the grand residences of former times (route 5) and the sleek skyscrapers of today (route 3), Sydney's urban fabric offers diverse delights.

RECOMMENDED ROUTES FOR...

ART LOVERS

Explore the shock of the new at the Museum of Contemporary Art (route 1), take a crash course in Australian art at the Art Gallery of NSW (route 2) or browse Paddington's private galleries (route 6).

CHILDREN

Let the kids run loose among the varied attractions of family-friendly Darling Harbour (route 4), marvel at the dinosaurs at the Australian Museum (route 1) or splash at some of Sydney's best-loved beaches (route 9).

FOOD AND DRINK

Sydney is a city of many flavours, so grab some Chinese dumplings (route 4), savour fish and chips by the harbour (route 8) or treat yourself to one of its trendy inner-city eateries (route 5).

GREEN SPACES

Enjoy the diverse charms of the harbourside Royal Botanic Gardens (route 2), the beaches and bushland of the Royal National Park (route 14) and the spectacular scenery of the Blue Mountains (route 13).

HISTORIANS

Get an insight into Australia's earliest days at The Rocks Discovery Museum (route 1), see how the colony's elite lived at Vaucluse House (route 7), and swot up on Captain Cook's landing at Botany Bay (route 10).

PHOTOGRAPHERS

Wait your turn with the wedding couples at Mrs Macquarie's Chair (route 2), shoot the length of the harbour from Watsons Bay (route 8) and get the clifftop perspective from the Bondi to Coogee Walk (route 9).

SWIMMERS

Savour the silence at Bungan Beach (route 12), discover your own pocket-sized strip of sand surrounded by bush on the Hermitage Foreshore Walk (route 7) and swim with groupers at Clovelly Beach (route 9).

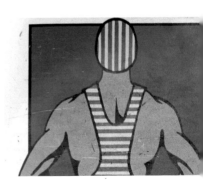

INTRODUCTION

An introduction to Sydney's geography, customs and culture, plus illuminating background information on cuisine, history and what to do when you're there.

EXPLORE SYDNEY

Welcome to the de facto capital of the Lucky Country – a fast moving modern metropolis built around a beautiful blue harbour. But Sydney is also an economic powerhouse, with a progressive arts scene and wonderfully close proximity to nature.

For most visitors, their Australian experience starts and ends in the seductive embrace of the Harbour City. Which is appropriate, because Sydney is Australia's first city in nearly all senses of the word. Canberra might be the modern capital, but Sydney was the first European settlement on the continent, remains the country's largest metropolis and its pulsing business and financial engine, and is home to its most recognisable manmade icons: the Harbour Bridge and Opera House.

BEGINNINGS

When you're staring star-struck at the magnificence of the Harbour Bridge and Opera house, or standing amid the glittering glass-and-concrete jungle of the Central Business District (CBD), it is easy to forget how young a city Sydney is. Just 240 years ago, it was little more than a few squalid huts clinging to the edge of the foreshore on The Rocks.

Indigenous people had inhabited the area in glorious isolation for around 45,000 years before a Yorkshireman arrived and ruined it all for them. Dutch explorers had touched on parts of the

Australian continent centuries before, but they saw little of value in the big brown land and it was left to Captain James Cook to 'discover' Sydney in 1770. He didn't hesitate to stick a flag in the land and claim it for king and country – setting a precedent that British backpackers still proudly observe on Bondi Beach to this day.

It took another 18 years before the first European settlement was created in 1788, with the arrival of the First Fleet under Captain Arthur Phillip, who tore up the original name (Albion) and christened the city after Lord Sydney, the British Home Secretary. Phillip only narrowly beat the French to the beach, though (see page 26).

Either way, the colonisers had landed and life was about to change dramatically for Australia's indigenous people. It's estimated that, prior to the arrival of the First Fleet, between 4,000 and 8,000 Aborigines lived in the region. They are commemorated in place names such as Cammeray (after the Cammeraygal tribe) and Ku-ring-gai (after the Gurringgai people).

The first settlers were a motley collection of convicts and soldiers. Syd-

A panoramic view of the downtown Sydney skyline

ney's early years were grim, with the colony nearly succumbing to starvation in 1790. In 1808, officers of the NSW Corps deposed luckless Governor Bligh (of Mutiny on the *Bounty* infamy) in the Rum Rebellion, but it wasn't until Governor Lachlan Macquarie arrived in 1810 that Sydney began its transformation into a colonial capital. It officially became a city in 1842.

Free settlers to the present day

Apart from some early structures at The Rocks, many of Sydney's most historic buildings date from Macquarie's time, including the grand buildings along Macquarie Street. His construction programme also included infrastructure such as roads, bridges and wharves, all of which were erected using the convenient convict labour force.

But, by 1830, free settlers were arriving in large numbers and convicts were outliving their sentences and being released into the growing community. The end of transportation in 1840 and the start of the Gold Rush in 1851 completely altered the dynamics of the colony, which had previously functioned more as a military outpost than an urban centre.

GEOGRAPHY AND LAYOUT

Today's population may be a relatively modest 4.5 million, but Sydney is not a small city. Its suburbs sprawl across the coastal basin, covering close to 2,000 sq km (1,240 sq miles), but easily the most defining feature of its geography is the harbour (comprising Port Jackson, which lies between North and South heads, Middle Harbour and North Harbour). The harbour divides the leafy north shore from the urban hub of the south, and provides many of the beaches and bays that are Sydneysiders' favourite playgrounds.

Central Sydney

The CBD stretches from the harbourside district of The Rocks, where Australia's first European colony was founded, south towards Central Station. It's a small area, with narrow Victorian streets that are fairly pedestrian-friendly (although watch out for the wing mirrors of the buses that race around this part of town, taking passengers but no prisoners in their vain attempt to keep to a timetable).

Traffic tends to grind to a standstill within the CBD, and during morning and evening peak hours (7–9am and 5–7pm), the problem extends in all directions. Exploring the city centre – the historic Rocks area, the museums and sights of the CBD and Hyde Park, the Royal Botanic Gardens, Sydney Harbour Bridge and the Sydney Opera House – is easily done on foot. Elsewhere, the inner-city neighbourhoods of Darlinghurst, Surry Hills, Paddington and Woollahra are particularly rewarding areas for a spot of urban strolling amid pretty Victorian terraces.

Looking across the water towards Sydney

New horizons

Developers in this city never sleep, and the skyline is set to change dramatically in the next few years. A whole new suburb has somehow been carved out right next to the Harbour Bridge, and Barangaroo – as it's known – will likely become well known name within a few years, with a trio of skyscrapers already being built, and several new outside areas and an entertainment/casino complex under heated discussion. A total of nine new cloud-skewering high-rise buildings of 200 metres or more in height will be casting long shadows across the city by 2020 if things go to plan.

Green dream

But Sydney remains close to nature. Near the city centre, on the fringes of the harbour foreshore near Rose Bay or Manly, you can find yourself ensconced in a bush landscape that the First Fleeters would recognise. Travel just a little further, to the Royal National Park in the south or the Blue Mountains to the west of the city, and you'll find raw landscapes that have remained utterly unaltered for thousands of years.

POPULATION

Sydney has a young and diverse populace. The controversial White Australia approach to immigration is, thankfully, long gone, and no more do the country's urban areas resemble British cities in the sun. The most striking feature for visitors from Europe and the US may be Sydney's vibrant Asian influence, with lots of locals having Chinese and Vietnamese heritage, and Southeast Asian cuisine being enormously popular. Given Australia's geographical location, this should not be too surprising.

In recent years, people have been arriving from Africa, the Middle East and elsewhere, adding fantastic flavour and colour to Sydney's increasingly rich multicultural mix. Occasionally there's a wobble – the ugly racially charged riots on the beaches of Cronulla in 2005 being one example – but broadly speaking the various communities get along well, as befits a city where everyone except a very small minority of Indigenous people are essentially

Arcades on Martin Place

Boomerangs

One of Australia's iconic mammals

immigrants (within a generation or so). The aftermath to the horrible hostage situation in Martin's Place in December 2014, when many Sydneysiders used social media to express their support for the local Muslim community amid fears of a backlash, exemplified the city's ethos.

Sydney is also accepting and supportive of its famously large gay and lesbian population, which is particularly visible in the inner-city areas of Darlinghurst and Newtown. The whole city is rightly proud of its legendary Mardi Gras, which usually happens in March.

CLIMATE

Sydney's temperate climate is one of its greatest assets, and a boon for visitors. Warm summers (December to February) are prevented from getting too hot by ocean breezes. Some travellers arrive

---

DON'T LEAVE SYDNEY WITHOUT...

Climbing the Coathanger. You haven't seen this city until you've gawped at it from atop the Sydney Harbour Bridge, 134 metres (440ft) up. Tours are available throughout the day and night. See page 39.

Getting some park life. Sydney's concrete jungle is punctuated by plenty of green spaces, including expansive Hyde Park and brilliant Botanical Gardens. To see some real Aussie bushland, explore the Royal National Park. See pages 35, 41 and 94.

Watching a movie under moonlight. For the ultimate nocturnal picnic, grab a rug and some cold beers and bag a spot of turf in front of a big screen at one of Sydney's alfresco cinemas. See page 23.

Enjoying a real break. Sydney has some of the best beaches of any city in the world, and they're all stroked by big Pacific breakers. Even if you don't attempt to surf, do explore this cracking coastline. See page 24.

Celebrating Christmas in July. Sydney never gets all that cold by European or north America barometers, but the Blue Mountains truly do shiver in the midwinter, even experiencing occasional snowfall. Join locals who head here to celebrate Yulefest – Christmas in July – complete with a traditional English Christmas dinner. See page 86.

Going hunting at the cellar door. Aussie wines are world beaters and just a couple of hours outside Sydney is the Hunter Valley, famed for full-bodied shiraz, fruity semillon and chardonnay. Sip wine amid the vines during a daytrip. See page 18.

Going for a paddle. The calm waters between The Spit and Manly are perfect for kayaking, and several local outfits offer kayak hire and tours, including the Manly Kayak Centre (www.manlykayakcentre.com.au) and Sydney Harbour Kayaks (www.sydneyharbourkayaks.com.au).

Sydney Harbour Bridge

completely unaware that Sydney gets a winter. It does, from June to August, and as 2015 proved, it can be quite bitter. In 'normal' years (if such things still exist), however, top temperatures rarely drop into single digits and rainfall remains relatively irregular – although dramatically torrid summer downpours do occasionally occur, and can be almost biblical in their rage when they happen (golf-ball sized hail stones have been known to fall).

The climate's most unpleasant characteristic is a tendency to humidity, particularly in February. Summer is the most popular season for tourists, and while it is a great opportunity to make the most of the city's great outdoors, you may get unpleasantly warm if you are rushing around trying to cram in lots of sights. Spring (September–November) and Autumn (March–May) are very comfortable seasons to be in Sydney.

LOCAL LIFE

The wonderful climate means that Sydneysiders spend a lot of their time outdoors: picnics, swims and barbecues after work are all important elements of the local social scene. Even when they go to restaurants and bars, alfresco options are a big draw. While Sydney has a big-city buzz, it is also slightly more laidback than many of its global counterparts. Business deals aplenty are made in this corporate capital, but the city lacks the frenetic vibe of places such as London and New York.

Sydneysiders have a passion for living well, which is seen in their dedication to fine dining as well as their penchant for enjoying the water that surrounds the city, whether it be swimming, sailing or simply taking a ride on a ferry. They also take pride in their burgeoning cultural scene, from pocket-sized art galleries and home-grown theatre, to big-name events at the Sydney Opera House, a symbol of the city's artistic ambitions.

There is a certain brash glamour to Sydney, just as there is in Rio or Los Angeles. With houses, bars and restaurants, it is all about the setting. Without that, the decor had better be sensational.

POLITICS AND ECONOMY

New South Wales missed out on much of the boom that buoyed the rest of Australia in the early 2000s (mostly driven by mining in Western Australia) and despite boasting the country's financial capital, its economy trailed the growth rate of other states.

After a record-setting four consecutive terms, the Labor Party were trounced in the 2011 New South Wales elections by the conservative Coalition of the Liberal and the National parties, who were then re-elected (albeit with a reduced majority) in 2015.

Pedestrians walking across the Pyrmont Bridge

TOP TIPS FOR VISITING SYDNEY

Pay first, travel later. All the buses along George Street are now prepay only, as are many other forms of transport. Get a ticket before you get on board (see page 133 for travel and ticket advice).

Midday oil. Australia has the highest rate of skin cancer in the world, so before you go out, remember to follow the mantra 'slip, slop, slap': slip on a shirt, slop on sunscreen and slap on a hat. If you go out without protection, you will undoubtedly burn.

Measure up. Sydney's pubs (often confusingly called hotels) serve beer in a bewildering range of measures, but the most common is the schooner, which can itself vary from 285 ml to 425ml… Whatever the measure, if someone 'shouts' you a beer, shout them one back.

Train spotting. Experience travelling across one of the wonders of the modern world on the cheap, by taking a train across the Sydney Harbour Bridge. Or walk it (see page 38).

Taxi! Sydney's taxis are notoriously expensive, 'premium services' charge even more, and the traffic can move slowly in the city centre. People newly arriving from a long flight can get stung. Get an idea of proper rates here: www.taxifare.com.au

Suburban sizzlers. Beach and backyard barbecues are a way of life for Sydneysiders, but you don't need a garden to cook up an alfresco storm – there are free barbecues in public parks and areas all over the city, including near the beaches.

In league. To have a meaningful conversation with a male Sydneysider, you're going to have to get into 'footy' – which means one thing here: rugby league. Ensconce yourself in a local pub and let a local explain the rules.

Wait for the green man. In Sydney it's illegal to jaywalk, ie to cross the road when you're not at a pedestrian crossing. This law is broken thousands of times a day, but occasionally police will pull people up for it, and you can be fined.

Welcome to the cheap seats. 'Tightarse Tuesday' is a wonderful concept whereby tickets to all kinds of shows, events and cinema screenings are discounted on Tuesday evenings.

Talking shop. Sydney shops tend to be open between 10am and 5pm Monday to Saturday, with shorter hours on Sundays. Thursday keeps late-night shopping hours, with many stores open until 9pm.

Crime stoppers. Sydney isn't especially dangerous, but it is a big city with its share of problems. Watch out for your bags when eating in places like Darling Harbour.

Don't get ripped. Bondi and its neighbouring beaches can be dangerous, with rips that carry swimmers out to sea, and occasional shark sightings. Follow basic beach rules: always swim between the flags, and if the shark alarm sounds, get out of the water at once.

The city is renowned for its superb seafood

FOOD AND DRINK

Sydney's dining scene is nothing short of sensational, with local chefs making the most of the city's fabulous fresh produce (including exceptional seafood) and culinary influences from its multicultural population to produce edible alchemy.

Perhaps the most surprising thing about Sydney's now internationally acclaimed restaurant scene is how recent it is. The first ethnic restaurants opened in the 1950s, and were run by immigrants for immigrants, Australians being highly suspicious of foreigners who did not eat at home like 'respectable folk'.

Once they tried it, however, Sydneysiders loved dining out, and a local cuisine quickly evolved, based on fresh local ingredients and techniques that married European and Asian traditions. 'Modern Australian' cooking is a fusion of the world's great traditional cuisines, particularly French, Italian, Chinese, Japanese, Vietnamese and Thai. The food tends to be fresh, light, low in fat, simply presented and reasonably priced.

'Bush tucker' – traditional plants and meats on which the indigenous Australians survived – makes occasional appearances on menus, with ingredients such as bush tomatoes, lemon myrtle and wattle seeds the most popular. But when Australians talk about 'real Aussie tucker', they probably mean items such as Vegemite (similar to Marmite), meat pies, and desserts such as Lamingtons (sponge cakes) and Pavlovas.

Organic food is growing in popularity, with a number of chefs deliberately choosing organic options. But it's the seafood that is the real show stopper. Sydney's love affair with local seafood – from fish such as snapper and John Dory to crustaceans including blue swimmer crabs and Balmain bugs – is nothing new. Archaeologists investigating Aboriginal middens have found deposits from Sydney rock oyster shells dating to 6,000 BC.

EATING OUT

The dinner rush in Sydney usually starts around 7pm and, except in a few late-night restaurants, most kitchens close around 10pm. If you are looking for a late-night feed, Chinatown remains your best bet. Tipping is totally optional – 10 percent is the standard for good service, but look out for service charges that might already be applied. By law, all restaurants are required to supply diners with tap water free of charge, if requested. Many restaurants close on Mondays.

Mushy peas on pie

Lamb chops on the barby

High-end restaurants

The undisputed star of Sydney's fine-dining scene is chef Tetsuya Wakada, whose French-Japanese fusion restaurant, Tetsuya's, consistently ranks among the world's best. That does not mean he has little competition: the likes of Neil Perry at the Spice Temple; Guillaume Brahimi at Guillaume in Paddington; Peter Doyle at est. and Kylie Kwong in her new pad at Potts Point all deliver food that is world-class. Sydney's best restaurants are generally easier to get into than those in London or New York, but you will still need to book ahead, particularly on a Friday or Saturday night.

Casual dining

While Sydneysiders love a touch of glamour they are, at heart, a rather casual breed, which is why the city has an abundance of relaxed eateries. Little distinction is made between brassieres and bistros, pub restaurants and cafés; anywhere that serves up quick and clever meals tends to be popular. Many such places are BYO, and most will take reservations.

Ethnic restaurants

Sydney's hundreds of ethnic restaurants reflect the country's changing immigration patterns. While Italian and Lebanese restaurants remain popular, it is not surprising that Asian restaurants dominate the ethnic dining scene, while African and Arabic-influenced fare is on the rise.

Chinatown's dozens of restaurants provide meeting places for the large Chinese community living in nearby high-rise units, with *yum cha*, similar to dim sum in Britain, being particularly popular. There is lots of Japanese cuisine on offer too, particularly at the ubiquitous sushi bars. However, Sydneysiders' most passionate long-standing love affair has been with Thai cuisine. Vietnamese cuisine, which shares a similar lightness and freshness, has been catching up recently.

Most ethnic restaurants are simple and unpretentious, but ethnic cuisine has also gone highbrow, with restaurants such as Longrain (Thai) and Billy Kwong (Chinese) taking it to new levels.

Cheap eats

Australia has myriad fast-food restaurants – the usual suspects, plus local chains such as Red Rooster for chicken and Hungry Jacks for burgers – but there are many other options for eating on a budget, including 'counter meals' at pubs. Cheap ethnic outlets and Asian-style food courts are always popular, but if you are in the mood for something hearty, the two mainstays of budget eating in the suburbs are the local Leagues Club (as in rugby league) and the RSL (Returned Servicemen's League). Both are open to non-members and offer unpretentious meal options and correspondingly good-value drinks. In town, try the NSW Leagues Club (www.nsw leaguesclub.com.au), Paddington RSL

Asian-style food is very popular

(www.paddorsl.com.au) or North Bondi RSL (www.northbondirsl.com.au), which also throws stunning views into the mix.

DRINKS

Alcohol has been a key theme in Australian life since the colony's earliest days. In 1808, on the 20th anniversary of the founding of New South Wales, members of the NSW Corps arrested and deposed Governor Bligh in what was Australia's first and only military coup – which flared up over the control of the young colony's most valuable commodity at the time: rum. Perhaps that is why the authorities have long tried to keep a firm hand on who gets to drink what, and when.

Until the 1950s, Sydney pubs were infamous for the 'six o'clock swill' (the rush for last drinks before the bar closed), and for segregated saloons for men and women. These days, licensing laws have eased considerably, but recent debates about 2am shutouts (when pubs stay open, but no new patrons are allowed in) have once again seen the government seeking to exert more control over the city's drinkers.

Wine

Australian wines are among the world's best, as international wine shows regularly confirm. Sauvignon blanc, Chardonnay and Semillon are the most favoured white varieties, while popular reds include Cabernet Sauvignon, Merlot, Pinot Noir and Shiraz (also known in Europe as Syrah). While areas such as the Hunter Valley (less than three hours' drive from Sydney), Barossa Valley, Yarra Valley and Margaret River have long enjoyed a good international reputation, Tasmanian wineries have also been getting attention of late, particularly for their Pinot Noir and Riesling.

Sparkling white wine – often served with a strawberry floater – is a common drink in bars and pubs. Many of Sydney's cheaper restaurants allow BYO (bring your own), although they may charge a 'corkage fee' – which can occasionally make it a less budget

---

Farmers' markets

In the last few years, local farmers' markets have increasingly become the place to buy gourmet produce, from boutique cheese to organic fruit and vegetables. Names to watch out for include Willowbrae cheese, Mandalong lamb and the Jannei goat dairy. The most central markets are the Good Living Growers' Market (Pyrmont Bay Park, opposite Star City Casino, first Sat of the month 7am–11am); Kings Cross Organic Food and Farmers' Market (Fitzroy Gardens, Kings Cross, second and fourth Sat of the month 9am–2pm); The Rocks Farmers' Market (Jack Mundey Place, corner of Argyle and George streets, The Rocks, Fri 10am–3pm).

Barbecued shrimps   *Local specialities*

option than it may appear. Wine is not sold in most supermarkets, but the city has plenty of bottle shops (off-licences), most of which offer a wide selection at very moderate prices. While Sydney has traditionally lagged behind Melbourne in the wine-bar stakes, the city now boasts a number of very good outlets, including The Winery (285a Crown Street, Surry Hills).

Beer

Like elsewhere in the beery regions of the planet, Australia has experienced an ale revolution in recent years. Gone are the days when most pubs only had a couple of taps, offering bog-standard lager. These days, alongside the older offerings such as Tooheys New, Carlton Draught and VB, you'll find all kinds of excellent locally brewed, smaller-batch pale ales and craft beers, including Two Birds, Kosciuszko IPA and Hangman Pale Ale, the latter cheerfully named after Alexander Green, executioner of Old Sydney Gaol for 27 years. Good beers brewed further afield include Boags and Cascade (from Tasmania) and Coopers (South Australia).

Australian beer is typically served very cold. Some beers are sold in 'new' and 'old' varieties, the first being lager, the latter darker in colour. The alcoholic strength of Australian beer must by law be displayed on the can or bottle. Full-strength draught beer is around 4.9 percent alcohol, 'mid-strength' beer will be around 3.5 percent alcohol, and beers that are marked 'light' will be no more than 2.7 percent alcohol.

Measures vary across Australia and are, frankly, confusing. In New South Wales, a 285ml (10-ounce) beer glass is called a 'middie' and a 425ml (15-ounce) glass is a 'schooner'. A small bottle of beer is known across Australia as a 'stubbie', and a box of 24 stubbies is a 'slab'. An off-licence is called a bottle shop, or 'bottle-o'. To 'shout' someone a drink means to buy them one, as in, 'Can I shout you a drink?' If someone 'shouts' you, drinking etiquette dictates you should 'shout' them in return.

Cocktails and spirits

The most famous Australian-made spirit is Bundaberg rum from Queensland, popularly ordered as 'Bundy and Coke'. It's not uncommon to see premixed rum and coke available on tap in pubs. However, a wide range of other spirits are offered in Australian bars, both straight or in cocktails, which in some bars are considered an art form.

Food and drink prices

Throughout this guide, we have used the following price ranges to show the average cost a two-course meal for one person with a glass of house wine:
$$$$ = over A$90
$$$ = A$70–90
$$ = A$50–70
$ = below A$50

Jeans at Sass & Bide

SHOPPING

Sydney offers plenty of retail therapy from unique and laidback markets to bustling malls, chic boutiques and elegant 19th–century arcades. Some neighbourhoods are defined by their stores, while the city centre offers one–stop shopping.

Like everywhere else, Sydney has felt the pinch as people increasingly shift to online shopping. However, the city has also discovered that properly bespoke and boutique outlets can't be replicated in the digital universe, so bricks and mortar shopping does still have a future. The burbs are full of smaller, more charismatic stores and studios, while the city's chief retail precinct and pedestrian area remains Pitt Street Mall.

THE ROCKS

The shops along George Street and hidden in the narrow side streets off it, specialise in all kinds of Australiana, from Aboriginal art and opal jewellery to individual knick-knacks available from the weekend market.

CBD

Sydney's two favourite department stores are a mere two blocks apart, both backing up against Market Street. Myer (436 George Street), the more 'accessible' store, sells everything from fashion to luggage and homewares. Its more upmarket rival, David Jones, covers similar ground, but with a more elegant fit-out and higher-end brands; it has two outlets diagonally opposite each other, the Market Street store (nos 65–77) stocking menswear, while the 'Elizabeth Street' store (actually at 86–108 Castlereagh Street) stocks womenswear. Sydney's best food hall is in the basement of the Market Street store.

Popular with beardy blokes and country girls, Bushman's outfitter R.M. Williams (389 George Street; www.rm williams.com.au) is famed for its riding boots and Akubra hats, which make great souvenirs.

Castlereagh Street is the place to find international luxury labels, including names such as Louis Vuitton (No. 63), Gucci (MLC Centre) and Chanel (No. 70).

Shopping centres

Pitt Street Mall (www.pittstreetmall.com. au) is lined with shopping centres, including Westfield (www.westfield.com.au/ sydney), and the nearby Galeries Victoria (www.thegaleries.com), which are both home to an array of small boutiques and chain stores. The elegant 19th-century Strand Arcade (www.strandarcade.com. au), which also opens onto Pitt Street

Aboriginal art   *Bondi logo on a lifeguard-red T-shirt*

Mall, houses a quality selection of top designers, while inside an extraordinarily beautiful 19th-century structure, the Queen Victoria Building (www.qvb.com.au), you will find many of the chain stores also represented in the Pitt Street Mall.

PADDINGTON

Paddington's leafy backstreets are home to many of the city's most fascinating small galleries, which specialise in Australian, Aboriginal and overseas artists. Absolutely fabulous fashionable and locally grown boutiques can be found on Glenmore Road and William Street (see Route 6), some of them genuinely world famous. Accessory stores, homeware shops and bookstores can be explored along Oxford Street and side streets.

SURRY HILLS

Surry Hills is traditionally where young designers open their first store, although some, such as celebrity favourite Wheels and Dollbaby (259 Crown Street; www.wheelsanddollbaby.com), never leave. South Dowling Street and Crown Street are good places to check out fresh talent.

WOOLLAHRA

If money is no object, look for antiques on Woollahra's leafy Queen Street, where an array of dealers specialise in clocks, jewellery, porcelain, silverware, glassware, books and maps.

Sydney's best markets

Saturday morning is market time. Glebe Market (Glebe Public School, Glebe Point Road; www.glebemarkets.com.au; Sat 9.30am–4.30pm) is the hippie market, where tarot card readers and incense stalls mix with quirky handmade clothing. The Rocks Market (George Street, Playfair Street & Jack Mundey Place; www.therocks.com/markets; Sat–Sun 10am–5pm) offers one-stop souvenir shopping, with unusual options such as vintage Australian travel posters. Paddington Markets (Paddington Uniting Church, 395 Oxford Street; www.paddingtonmarkets.com.au; Sat 10am–4pm) is deservedly Sydney's most famous market, with over 250 different stalls; it is *the* place to catch up-and-coming designers. Paddy's Markets (corner of Thomas and Hay streets, Haymarket; www.paddysmarkets.com.au; Fri–Sun 9am–5pm) is a confusing jumble of cheap and cheerful stalls selling everything from goldfish and toys to fresh fruit. Bondi Market (Bondi Beach Public School, Bondi Beach; www.bondimarkets.com.au; Sun 10am–4pm) offers vintage clothing, handmade soaps and vinyl records, while the Surry Hills Markets (Shannon Reserve, corner Crown and Collins streets; first Saturday of every month) have a community feel, with stalls selling handmade, second-hand and recycled goods.

The city has a thriving theatre scene

ENTERTAINMENT

From live music and outdoor performances to glamorous harbourside venues, theatres in converted stables and clubs that bounce into the small hours – Sydney has a thumping, diverse entertainment scene that caters to every proclivity.

Traditionally, Melbourne is seen as the country's custodian of the arts, while Sydney is portrayed as being more interested in froth than substance, but perceptions are changing. Fretting about the state of the arts is something of an obsession for Australians of a certain class, and it's true that government funding is not always brilliant. Flagship arts companies have had to be bailed out more than once and, in the past, the film industry has lurched from one crisis to another – although several Australia-based film companies regularly deliver top-quality work.

THEATRE

Sydney's two high-profile theatre companies have long had distinctly contrasting reputations. The Sydney Theatre Company (STC), with its harbourside home, has traditionally attracted major sponsors, while Company B at Belvoir Street, nestled in an inner-city backstreet, has received less money but more critical acclaim. However, the appointment in 2008 of Cate Blanchett and her playwright husband Andrew Upton, as co-artistic directors of the STC, saw the company pick up some kudos points;

Blanchett moved on in 2012 and Upton stepped down in late 2015, replaced by esteemed British theatre director, Jonathan Church. Meanwhile, smaller companies such as the Griffin Theatre Company continue to be a crucible for new work.

DANCE

Australia's dance scene is small, with just three major companies – the Australian Ballet, the Sydney Dance Company and Bangarra Dance Theatre – each committed to showcasing new work. Both the Australian Ballet, under artistic director David McAllister, and Bangarra, under artistic director Stephen Page, enjoy international reputations.

The Sydney Dance Company had a difficult time after the departure of founder Graeme Murphy in 2007. Prodigious young talent Tanja Liedtke was tragically killed in an accident on the eve of taking over as Artistic Director and it wasn't until 2009 that Barcelona-born Rafael Bonachela took the post. In the six years that he's been at the helm, the company has re-established itself as the country's premier contemporary dance company.

Sydney is a great place to catch live music

MUSIC

Rock and pop

Sydney has various venues that support live music, from the big, like the Metro (www.metrotheatre.com.au) and Enmore (www.enmoretheatre.com.au), to the small, such as the brilliantly named Goodgod Small Club (www.goodgodgoodgod.com) – plus plenty of in-betweeners. The city has produced a wealth of world-class rock, pop, electronic and indie bands over the years, from Midnight Oil and INXS through the Vines, the Presets, Angus & Julia Stone, and Sneaky Sound System, to contemporary acts like Cloud Control.

Classical music and jazz

The Sydney Symphony Orchestra, the city's resident orchestra, welcomed a new artistic director, American conductor David Robertson, in 2014. Like Opera Australia, the orchestra use the Opera House as their Sydney base, leaving the City Recital Hall as the venue of choice for other ensembles such as the Australian Chamber Orchestra and the Brandenburg Orchestra.

Sydney's jazz scene is small but enthusiastic, with The Basement being the most respected and long-running venue.

FILM

Sydney has produced and/or nurtured some serious acting talent (Nicole Kidman, Hugh Jackman, Bryan Brown, Russell Crowe, Sam Worthington, Toni Collette, Rose Byrne et al) and directors including Baz Luhrman. The country also frequently reprises its role as a preferred film set location, with a plethora of big-budget Hollywood blockbusters being shot on Australian shores, including the new *Pirates of the* Caribbean flicks (during the filming of which, Johnny Depp got into hot water for smuggling his dogs into the country illegally).

CINEMA

There are various multiplexes around the city, and several good quality arthouse cinemas, including the historic Hayden Orpheum (www.orpheum.com.au). During summer, cult, classic and new films are screened at various moonlit cinema venues, including the Botanical Gardens and Bondi Beach – see www.openaircinemas.com.au/sydney for more.

NIGHTLIFE

Sydney has no shortage of watering holes, from small wine bars to pumping clubs. Areas such as King Street Wharf are popular with 20-somethings. Venues range from the mega, like Marquee (www.marqueesydney.com), through to places that showcase serious local talent on the turntables, such as the Chinese Laundry (www.chineselaundryclub.com.au).

Be sure to swim safely

THE GREAT OUTDOORS

From the beach to the bush, Sydneysiders are spoiled for choice when it comes to nature's playground. To get a real feel for this aspect of city life, slap on a hat, slop on some sunscreen and head outside.

When the sun's out, Sydneysiders head to the beach to go surfing and swimming, or hit the harbour for a spot of yachting, kayaking or simply to go walking around the coast. Don't worry if you're not a water baby, though – there are numerous ways to explore Sydney's most iconic landscapes.

Whatever outdoor activities you indulge in, don't forget to cover up with sun screen and a hat – the sun is extremely strong down under and incidents of skin cancer are high.

BEACHES

Sydney has over 70 harbour and ocean beaches, most of which are patrolled by volunteer lifesavers. The harbour beaches, such as Balmoral in the north and Nielsen Park in the east, have calm waters and are popular with families and snorkellers. Ocean beaches, like Bondi and Manly, are a magnet for surfers and strong swimmers.

Many of Sydney's ocean beaches are prone to rips or strong currents, so always swim with care. At surf beaches, lifesavers will erect red-and-yellow flags; the zone between the flags is the safe swimming zone. If there's a sign saying the beach is closed, do not even think about swimming – lifesavers will not close a beach unless conditions are truly treacherous, so you would be putting their life at risk, as well as yours.

ISLANDS

The islands of Sydney Harbour form part of the Sydney Harbour National Park, and many of them are open to visitors. The easiest to access is Fort Denison, the tiny fortified outcrop just beyond Circular Quay, from where a regular ferry service runs. Daily tours cover the fascinating history of the island, which was used as place of punishment before it was fortified around the time of the Crimean War, due to fear of attack from the Russians.

There are also daily ferry services to the largest harbour island, Cockatoo Island, where you can take self-guided tours of various landmarks, including a former shipbuilding site and a convict prison. You can even pitch a tent and spend a night on the island.

Leafy Royal National Park   *One of the city's many sandy beaches*

If all you're after is a picnic on the harbour, Rodd Island, Clark Island and Shark Island are all open to visitors, but Shark Island is the only one served by a regular ferry. For more information on visiting the harbour islands, contact the Sydney Harbour National Park Information Centre (tel: 9247 5033; www.nationalparks.nsw.gov.au).

NATIONAL PARKS

Sydney is surrounded by several national parks that are close enough to be visited on a day trip. To the south, the Royal National Park – Australia's oldest – has varied landscapes, from bush to heath, as well as magnificent beaches. However, the Blue Mountains National Park (see page 86) remains one of the city's most popular getaways, thanks to its spectacular landscapes and charming towns. A trip here reveals a very different landscape to Sydney's city and beaches.

WALKS

You do not have to head out of town to enjoy a good bushwalk; Sydney has plenty of pockets of urban bushland that make for a pleasant stroll, as well as some spectacular cliff walks. Three of the best are outlined in detail in this book. The short Hermitage Foreshore Walk (see page 66) is an easy, accessible trail, as is the South Head Walk (see page 68). Both these routes enjoy spectacular harbour views. If you like a more challenging trek, the Bondi to Coogee Walk (see page 72) is a robust clifftop hike on the oceanside, while the Spit to Manly walk (see page 80) takes in magnificent bushland as well as more refined urban surroundings.

Terror of the deep

With place names such as Shark Island and Shark Point, and several beaches equipped with shark nets, you would be forgiven for wondering what your chances are of encountering Jaws in the waters around Sydney. The short answer is slim. While sharks are regularly spotted in harbour waters, there has not been a fatal shark attack in Sydney harbour since 1963 – although a navy diver was very badly injured by a bull shark in 2009. Popular beaches such as Bondi, Bronte and Tamarama are subject to shark patrols, and if patrollers are concerned about a shark's proximity, they will clear the waters. On the other hand, it is true that shark numbers have been increasing in recent years, due to cleaner waters and more food, and some experts say that it is just a matter of time until the creatures become more invasive. The best advice is to take sensible precautions, such as avoiding swimming in murky waters or near river/drain outlets.

Captain Cook's ship Endeavour aground on the Great Barrier Reef, by William Byrne

HISTORY: KEY DATES

In the 240 years since the first Europeans arrived, Sydney has seen many seismic changes: what started as a straggling penal settlement has evolved into one of the world's leading cities.

FIRST SETTLEMENT

AD 1770	Captain James Cook lands at Botany Bay and claims the east coast of Australia for the British Crown.
1778	The First Fleet arrives from England under the command of Captain Arthur Phillip, bringing 736 convicts. A prison camp is set up in Sydney Cove.
1789	The first convict is hanged for murdering a fellow-prisoner. Skirmishes with Aborigines. Smallpox epidemic among Aborigines.
1790	The ill-equipped Second Fleet arrives; the colony nearly succumbs to starvation.
1793	Free settlers arrive in the colony; ex-convict James Ruse sets up the first farm in Parramatta.

COLONIAL CAPITAL

1808	NSW Corps depose Governor Bligh in the Rum Rebellion
1810	Governor Lachlan Macquarie begins to transform Sydney from a penal settlement to a colonial capital.
1815	Explorers Blaxland, Wentworth and Lawson find a route over the Blue Mountains, heralding Sydney's commercial expansion.
1830s	Free settlers begin to arrive in large numbers.
1840	Transportation of convicts to Sydney is abolished.
1850	The University of Sydney is founded.

GOLD RUSH ERA

1851	Gold is discovered in the Blue Mountains, sparking Australia's first Gold Rush.

Building the Sydney Harbour Bridge, which opened in 1932

1880	Sydney hosts the southern hemisphere's first World Fair.
1900	Bubonic plague results in large areas of Sydney's The Rocks area being razed.

20TH CENTURY

1901	The states join together to become the Commonwealth of Australia. Melbourne is the temporary capital, but Sydney insists that a new capital, Canberra, be built between the two.
1914–18	World War I. Australia suffers high casualties.
1919	Spanish influenza kills more people in Sydney than the war.
1932	Sydney Harbour Bridge opens.
1939–45	Sydneysiders enlist again to fight in Europe in World War II.
1942	Japan threatens Australia. Three midget submarines in Sydney Harbour spark panic.
1961	The last trams are removed from Sydney's streets. The first skyscrapers are built in the city.
1971	The first 'green bans' are imposed by the Builders' Labourers Federation to save historic properties from demolition.
1973	Sydney Opera House opens.
1978	The first Gay and Lesbian Mardi Gras parade ends in violence after the police attack participants.
1988	Sydney is the focus of celebrations for Australia's bicentenary. Aborigines campaign for land rights.
2000	Sydney hosts a successful Olympic Games.
2006	Sydney is covered in smoke after raging fires in the Blue Mountains.
2008	The Federal government apologises to Aborigines for past wrongs.
2010	Julia Gillard, a Welsh-born Australian, becomes the first female prime minister of Australia.
2011	After a record-setting four terms, Labor lose state elections to conservative Coalition of Liberal and Nationals
2013	Tony Abbott, leader of the Liberal Party, becomes prime minister.
2014	A lone gunman takes 18 people hostage in Sydney's Martin Place. Three people die in the resulting shootout.
2015	The Coalition wins re-election, but Abbott loses a snap leadership vote and is replaced as PM by Malcolm Turnbull. Mike Baird becomes NSW premier.

BEST ROUTES

Queen Victoria Building

CITY CENTRE HIGHLIGHTS

This tour takes you through 240 years of Sydney's history, from The Rocks – where the fledgling colony began – to the 21st-century heart of the Central Business District (CBD), with the chance to do a bit of shopping thrown in.

DISTANCE: 7km (4.5 miles)
TIME: A full day
START: Sydney Visitor Centre
END: Australian Museum
POINTS TO NOTE: This tour is best done at the weekend if you want to catch The Rocks Market in full swing. The distance noted above is for the route drawn in red on the map but doesn't include the bus trip in between.

One of Sydney's main tourist areas, The Rocks is buzzing by day, alive with people wandering around its shops, sights, cafes, pubs and restaurants. To the south, the Central Business District (CBD) includes soaring buildings, Victorian landmarks and Hyde Park.

THE ROCKS

To the west of Circular Quay is the area known as The Rocks, a sandstone peninsula where the First Fleet stumbled ashore after an eight-month voyage and set about building a colony. Originally, it comprised a ragged jumble of wharves and warehouses, hovels, brothels, pubs and shops; by the late 19th century, it had become a slum of seedy houses and pubs. An outbreak of bubonic plague early in the 1900s led to a government clean up and the demolition of the worst of the buildings.

Another spate of demolition occurred in the 1920s, to make room for the approaches to the Harbour Bridge, which opened in 1932. In the 1960s, it was proposed to level the area entirely to make way for a mini-Manhattan; the plan was defeated when residents enlisted the support of building unions, who placed 'green bans' on the work. From the 1970s the emphasis was on preservation and renovation, but in 2014 plans were mooted for knocking down old housing around Millers Point and replacing them with a 'millionaire's paradise', while a controversial new casino is planned for nearby Barangaroo. Watch this space.

Sydney's CBD   *George Street*

Sydney Visitor Centre

West of Circular Quay is the starting point of this route, the **Sydney Visitor Centre ❶** (corner of Argyle and Playfair streets; tel: 1800 067 676; www.shfa. nsw.gov.au; daily 9.30am–5.30pm). Staff are very helpful here, and you can stock up on local info brochures and maps.

The Rocks Discovery Museum

Go downstairs, walk to the far end of the building and exit to the right to find **The Rocks Discovery Museum ❷** (Kendall Lane; www.therocks.com; daily 10am–5pm; free). This small museum provides an excellent introduction to the area's indigenous inhabitants, the early days of the colony, and how it has evolved. If

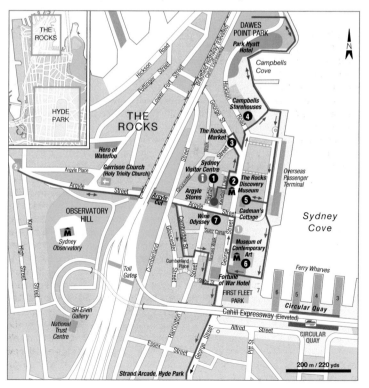

Cadman's Cottage

you can, look out of the back door of the museum to peep at the tiny backyards and courtyards of the kind that once predominated in this part of town.

The Rocks Market

Turn right out of the front of the museum on to Kendall Lane and follow this road on to George Street, which is the oldest European road on the Australian continent, and can be seen on maps dating back as far as 1791. Turn left to hit **The Rocks Market ❸** (George and Playfair streets; www.therocks.com; Sat–Sun 10am–5pm), although please note it is open at weekends only. There's a plethora of stalls here, selling wares from jewellery to craft items such as fruit bowls carved from native hardwoods.

After spending time at the market, pick up Hickson Road briefly, before turning right, down to the water. To your left are the impressive **Campbells Storehouses ❹**, named after trader Robert Campbell, who built them in 1838. These days they house a number of restaurants.

Follow the path north along the water, past the five-star Park Hyatt Hotel, which has some of the best views in Sydney, to the pretty park on **Dawes Point**, a scenic spot that's popular for wedding photos.

Cadman's Cottage

Retracing your steps, follow the waterfront back towards Circular Quay. After you pass the high-end restaurants housed in the Overseas Passenger Terminal on your right, you will come to **Cadman's Cottage ❺** (110 George Street; Tue–Sun 10am–4.30pm; free), the oldest residence in central Sydney, and the only one that gives a feel for the simple constructions of the colony's early days. It was built in 1816 to house the governor's coxswain and crew, and is named after John Cadman, the last coxswain to live there. The building originally fronted onto a sandy beach, but due to land reclamation it's now set well back from the water.

Museum of Contemporary Art

Past Cadman's Cottage, on your right as you hug the waterfront, is the massive Art Deco bulk of the **Museum of Contemporary Art ❻** (140 George Street; www.mca.com.au; daily 10am–5pm; free). The museum has a permanent collection of Australian, modern Aboriginal and international art, and hosts a variety of excellent temporary exhibitions. It also has a good gift shop.

By now you'll probably be in need of refreshment – luckily there are plenty of options on George Street. About 50 metres north of the museum, some of the best Thai food in Sydney can be sampled at the stylish **Sailor's Thai** eatery, see ❶.

Wine Odyssey

For more liquid refreshment, cross George Street, take the first left at Argyle Street and opposite the Visi-

Pulling a pint in the historic Lord Nelson

tor Centre find **Wine Odyssey ⑦** (corner of Harrington and Argyle streets; www.wineodyssey.com.au; Sun–Wed noon–10pm, Thur–Sat noon–midnight; charge). This wine bar and education centre brings some of Australia's lesser-known wines to a broader audience. On offer are tastings of 50 handpicked wines that are usually only available to the public at the cellar door. In the Aroma Room you can take in 50 wine smells, while in the Tasting Theatre you can learn about six of Australia's best niche wineries. The shop sells more than 400 wines by the bottle, and there is also an à la carte restaurant.

Argyle Cut

If beer is more to your taste, take a detour and head west up Argyle Street through the Argyle Cut, a massive tunnel carved out by convicts. As you emerge, the **Garrison Church** is on your right and **Observatory Hill** to your left. Continue west for another block and you will reach the **Lord Nelson Brewery Hotel**, see ②. This atmospheric sandstone hotel is one of the oldest pubs in The Rocks and it brews a range of beers on site.

Head back down Argyle Street, through the Cut and take the first turning on your right, Cambridge Street, which will lead you into a warren of narrow, atmospheric streets that were once typical of the area. Follow the signs for the Mission Stairs to Nurses Walk, then turn right, and walk 50 metres before turning left on Globe Street towards George Street.

CBD

From here, hop on any of the buses heading south (right) along George Street (note: you need a prepaid ticket) and ask to be let out at the Strand Arcade in the heart of the Central Business District (CBD).

Strand Arcade

The **Strand Arcade ⑧** (412 George Street; www.strandarcade.com.au) is one of Sydney's architectural gems, with tiered mezzanines and decorative ironwork. Connecting George and Pitt streets, it houses a variety of boutiques on the first and second floors (check out local designers such as Leona Edmiston and Alannah Hill), as well as a collection of appealing cafes, including **Pendolino**, see ③.

Sydney Tower

Walk through the Strand Arcade and emerge on to the Pitt Street Mall, Sydney's pedestrian shopping zone. Head south and enter the **Westfield Sydney shopping centre** (www.westfield.com.au/sydney; stores Mon–Sat 9am–6.30pm, Sun 10am–6pm) on your left for the **Sydney Tower Eye ⑨** (Podium Level; www.sydneytowereye.com.au; summer daily 9am–10pm, summer daily 9am–9.30pm; charge), the tallest structure in Sydney. From the observation deck, 250 metres (820ft) above street level, you can enjoy 360-degree views of the city. Or, if you like an

Strand Arcade

adrenalin rush, buy a Skywalk ticket to traverse the outdoor walkways and glass-floor overhangs at the top of the tower. Your ticket includes a seat in the 4D Cinema Experience, which transports you across Sydney Harbour, over the city's incredible coastline and iconic landmarks, with the fourth dimension provided by in-theatre effects including wind, bubbles and fire.

Queen Victoria Building

Exit on Pitt Street and walk west down Market Street for one block to reach the **Queen Victoria Building** ❿ (QVB; 455 George Street; www.qvb.com.au; Mon–Wed and Fri–Sat 9am–6pm, Thur 9am–9pm, Sun 11am–5pm), which occupies an entire block of George Street between Market and Druitt streets. Opened in 1898 to celebrate Queen Victoria's golden jubilee, the building, which once housed tradespeople, showrooms and a concert hall, was built on the site of a street market and fell into neglect before being entirely refurbished in 1986, as a three-storey shopping arcade. A second (A$35.5 million) refurbishment, completed in 2009, has enhanced its

exquisite 19th-century interiors, which include leadlight wheel windows and original floor tiles.

Sydney Town Hall

Emerging at the Druitt Street end of the QVB, cross the road to **Sydney Town Hall** ⓫ (483 George Street; Mon–Fri 9am–6pm; free), a sandstone building in the Victorian style. Interior highlights include the stunning Vestibule Room, which features magnificent stained glass and a massive crystal chandelier, and the Centennial Hall, dominated by

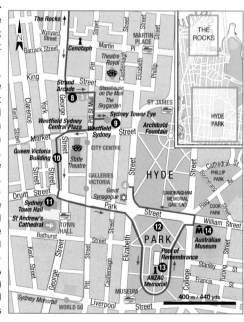

Queen Victoria Building　　　　　*The Archibald Fountain in Hyde Park*

the largest tubular-pneumatic organ ever built, with around 8,700 pipes. Free organ recitals are held regularly.

HYDE PARK

Head east up Park Street (the extension of Druitt Street) for three blocks and you will reach **Hyde Park** ⓬ on Elizabeth Street. Named after London's famous green space, it was originally used as a racecourse but is now divided into two halves by Park Street. An impressive boulevard of trees runs through the centre of its northern end, opening onto the 1932 **Archibald Fountain**, a neo-classical bronze-and-granite design by French sculptor François Sicard, which commemorates the alliance of Australian and French forces in World War I. Just near the corner of Park and College streets, in the sunken Sandringham Memorial Gardens, is a pergola that becomes a cascade of flowering wisteria in September.

At the south end of the park, the Art Deco **ANZAC Memorial and Pool of Remembrance** ⓭ (www.anzacmemorial. nsw.gov.au; daily 9am–5pm; free) was erected in 1934, to commemorate the troops from New South Wales who served in World War I.

AUSTRALIAN MUSEUM

Head back up to Park Street and cross College Street. Opposite the south end of Hyde Park is the **Australian Museum** ⓮ (6 College Street; www.australian museum.net.au; daily 9.30am–5pm; charge). Established in 1827, it is Australia's oldest museum and enjoys an international reputation in the fields of natural history and indigenous research. It's a great place to learn about Australia's unique flora, fauna and cultures.

Dinosaurs
Start on the top floor of the three-storey building, where two of the most popular exhibits are found. The Dinosaurs exhibit is a favourite with kids of all

Observatory Hill

Observatory Hill, off Argyle Street, is the highest natural point in the city, and has at various times housed a windmill (1796), then a half-built fort (1803) and a shipping signal station (1848). Today it is home to two notable museums: the Sydney Observatory (Watsons Road, Observatory Hill; tel: 9921 3485; www.sydneyobservatory.com.au; daily 10am–5pm and evenings Apr–Mar; charge), which has a 3-D space theatre and a planetarium, as well as some impressive telescopes; and the S.H. Ervin Gallery. Housed within the National Trust Centre, the gallery (Watsons Road, Observatory Hill; www.nationaltrust. com.au; Tue–Sun 11am–5pm; charge) has a very good collection of Australian figurative art.

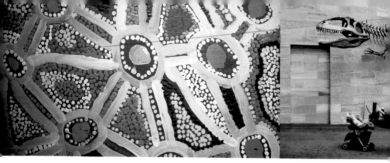

Aboriginal art...

ages, with the highlights being the 10 complete skeletons and eight life-size models. Some of Australia's distinctive dinosaurs are on display, including **Eric the Pliosaur**. Found in the opal-mining town of Coober Pedy, Eric is unique in that during the fossilisation process, his entire skeleton was replaced with opal.

Australian fauna

On the same floor is **Surviving Australia**, a fabulous exhibition devoted to Australia's unique fauna, from Tasmanian devils and platypuses to deadly spiders and snakes (the 10 most venomous snakes in the world are all found in Australia). The exhibit is divided into sections dealing with separate habitats, including a section on the animals that can be found in both urban and suburban environments. Also enthralling is the exhibit devoted to extinct fauna, including six species of marsupial lion, which weighed up to 160kg (350lbs).

Skeletons and minerals

If you have under-5s with you, duck into **Kidspace**, where children can get hands-on with artefacts as well as playing with puzzles, puppets and dressing-up clothes. Alternatively, head down to the first floor to inspect a dazzling collection (one of the world's best) of multicoloured minerals, before continuing down to the ground floor where the skeleton gallery fascinates visitors of all ages. Favourite exhibits include Jumbo the elephant and the Bone Ranger, a human skeleton sitting on a skeletal horse.

Indigenous Australians

Also on this floor is the museum's other key attraction, a fascinating section devoted to Indigenous Australians, and featuring 40,000 different exhibits representing the diverse experience of Aborigines and Torres Strait Islanders. This culture, which included around 700 language groups, flourished for over 40,000 years before the Europeans arrived. Learn about The Dreaming, which forms the basis of much of Aboriginal spirituality, and examine Aboriginal art that has attracted enormous interest around the world in recent decades.

Historical events and politics are also addressed, including the 1960s Freedom Rides – inspired by the US Civil Rights Movement – and the Stolen Generations. Between the late 1800s and the 1970s, some 100,000 indigenous children were taken from their families and placed in white homes or institutions – behaviour that shocked Australia when it became the subject of a national inquiry in 1997. In 2000, 250,000 people marched across the Sydney Harbour Bridge to call for reconciliation and a national apology, which did not come until February 2008, when new Labor Prime Minister Kevin Rudd made it one of his first official acts.

To finish off a long day, walk back across the park to Elizabeth Street and enjoy a quiet drink in one of the city's

Dinosaur skeleton...   *...and exterior, all at the Australian Museum*

nicest wine bars, **Bambini Trust Wine Room**, see ④.

Watering Holes

If you discover you've walked up a thirst, The Rocks has many pubs – including some of Sydney's oldest and most storied watering holes – where you can remedy that situation. Aside from the Lord Nelson, try the Fortune of War Hotel (137 George Street): beer has been served on this site since 1839. Another great alternative is the Hero of Waterloo (81 Lower Fort Street), where the cellars were reportedly used as holding cells for press-ganged sailors.

Food and drink

① SAILOR'S THAI AND SAILOR'S THAI CANTEEN

106 George Street, The Rocks; tel: 9251 2466; www.sailorsthai.com.au; Mon–Fri noon–3pm & 5pm–10pm, Sat–Sun 5pm–10pm; $$–$$$

There are two options here to suit different budgets, both of which deliver sensational Thai tucker. At street level is the lower-priced option, a canteen with a communal table and open kitchen in the newer part of the building; downstairs, the restaurant is housed in an old sandstone sailors' home on the waterfront, and is an atmospheric place for a weekday lunch or dinner.

② LORD NELSON BREWERY HOTEL

19 Kent Street, The Rocks; 02 9251 4044; www.lordnelsonbrewery.com; bar: Mon–Sat 11am–11pm, Sun noon–10pm; brasserie: Thurs–Fri noon–3pm, Tue–Sat 6pm–10pm; $$

One of The Rocks' true treasures, this sandstone pub has been serving beer since 1831, although the current name dates back to 1841. Try one of the six beers brewed on site along with some pub fare, or enjoy quality dining in Nelson's Brassiere upstairs.

③ PENDOLINO

Level 2, Strand Arcade, George Street, Sydney; tel: 9231 6117; www.pendolino. com.au; Mon–Sat 12pm–3pm, 6pm–late; $$

This sexy space at the top of the Strand Arcade is the place to come for fabulous regional Italian cuisine. If you're not in the mood for a meal, the adjacent café offers delicious breakfasts, before reinventing itself as a wine bar in the evening.

④ BAMBINI TRUST WINE ROOM

185 Elizabeth Street; tel: 9283 7098; www.bambinitrust.com.au; Mon–Fri 7am–late, Sat 5.30pm–late; $$

This exquisite little Parisian-style bar has an extensive list of wines by the glass, including European options and a diverse Australian selection. Nibbles include whisky-cured salmon gravlax with remoulade and rye. For a more substantial meal, book at the classy restaurant.

Sydney Harbour Bridge

HARBOUR HIGHLIGHTS

Sydney's two great icons, the Harbour Bridge and the Opera House, kick off this walk, which then takes in nearby foreshore must-sees on the south side, including the Royal Botanic Gardens.

DISTANCE: 8km (5 miles)
TIME: A full day
START: Sydney Harbour Bridge
END: Woolloomooloo
POINTS TO NOTE: If it's a nice day, pack your swimming costume; you can take a dip either before commencing the route in North Sydney or at the Andrew (Boy) Charlton Pool (see page 42).

Sydney's harbour is the focal point for the city, and this route takes in the best of the central foreshore. Starting on the North Shore, it crosses the Harbour Bridge, wends its way to the Opera House and through the Royal Botanic Gardens to the Art Gallery of NSW, finishing in the former working-class enclave of Woolloomooloo.

SYDNEY HARBOUR BRIDGE

It is hard to imagine the city without the celebrated **Sydney Harbour Bridge ❶**, which opened in 1932 and was for a long time the world's largest single-span bridge. Before it opened, up to 40 million passengers a year crossed the water by ferry. These days, the bridge is supplemented by a tunnel, which still has heavy traffic flows in peak hour. The A$20 million bridge took 1,400 workers nine years to construct, and cost 16 of them their lives. It has eight lanes, two rail lines, a footpath and a cycle path.

The opening ceremony was famously disrupted when, as a political statement against the socialist government, eccentric Irishman Francis de Groot galloped forward on a horse and slashed the ribbon with his sword, declaring the bridge open 'in the name of the decent citizens of New South Wales'. De Groot was removed, the ribbon tied back together, and the ceremony continued.

There are four ways to cross the bridge: take the train, cycle, walk or drive – note: it's a toll road. To walk (it's a 30-minute stroll), catch the train to Milson's Point station, exit to the east and climb the sandstone stairs leading to the footpath that runs the

The iconic Opera House

span of the bridge. If you tackle the 200 steps to the top of the south-eastern pylon, you will be rewarded with a museum telling the story of the bridge's history, and get a bird's eyeful of Sydney from a viewing platform.

Those with a head for heights might want to try a very different kind of walk – right across the top of the iconic Coathanger (as the bridge is affectionately known to locals). People have been climbing Sydney Harbour Bridge for years, but it has only been legal since 1998, and now you have to pay to do it. **Bridgeclimb** (www.bridgeclimb.com) organises three-and-a-half-hour tours of the bridge, culminating at the apex of the arch, 134

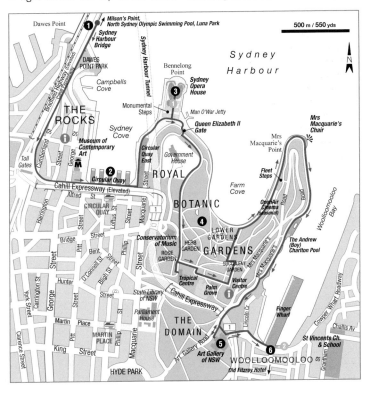

The view from Harbour Bridge

metres (440ft) above harbour level. Four tours are available: during the day and night, and at sunset and sunrise. Note: you will be breathalysed before being allowed to climb.

CIRCULAR QUAY

At the southern end of the bridge are stairs running down to The Rocks (see page 30), but to continue this route, walk up another flight of steps and continue on the walkway that runs east alongside the Cahill Expressway. After 10–15 minutes, you will come to a lift that goes down to **Circular Quay** ❷, which is always crowded with a mix of commuters and tourists being raucously entertained by buskers. Large plaques along the quay are part of a Writers' Walk honouring famous Australian authors, giving details of their careers and works (for details about some of Sydney's scribes, see page 136).

Walk east along the quay towards Bennelong Point and the Opera House. East Circular Quay – a mix of residences, boutiques, restaurants and bars – was developed in the run-up to the millennium, and was at first hugely controversial. When the 1960s office blocks that had stood on the site were torn down, Sydneysiders got used to the open space, and they protested strongly when the apartment building known as The Toaster was developed. However, it has now become part of the city fabric.

SYDNEY OPERA HOUSE

Sydney Opera House ❸ (Bennelong Point; www.sydneyoperahouse.com; entry free, tours and events charge) was designed by Danish architect Jørn Utzon – who stormed out before it was finished, and has never seen the building since. The complex and controversial structure took 14 years to complete and was fraught with problems. It finally opened in 1973, and today it's the city's most popular building. In addition to operas and symphony concerts, it hosts drama, comedy, contemporary music and experimental performances (see page 118), and events are regularly held on the forecourt, where the stone stairs double as seating. It's the scene of a mass gathering at New Years Eve, when thousands come to watch fireworks set fire to the sky over the bridge. Interestingly, it was a place of celebration for the Eora people (who called the site Tjubagali) long before Europeans arrived. A large midden site of white cockleshells (the name means 'white mud clay') also has a curious parallel with the modern-day structure.

Spectacular design

The design's most striking features are the sail-like structures, suggestive of yachts on the harbour; these are covered with a million anti-fungal tiles and weigh 158,000 tonnes. A num-

Cacti in the Royal Botanic Gardens

ber of engineering and financial problems forced the government to scale the project down from Utzon's original vision, leading the architect to resign. Nevertheless, the budget (originally A$7 million) topped A$102 million by the end.

Concerts and performances

Queen Elizabeth II opened the Opera House in 1973. The first production in the intimate Opera Theatre was Prokofiev's *War and Peace*, while in the Concert Hall it was Beethoven's Ninth Symphony. Today, more than 3,000 performances and events are held here annually.

The Opera House has several restaurants: the casual **Mozart Café**, popular **Opera Bar**, see ➊, and a fine-dining option at **Bennelong**, where celebrated Australian chef Peter Gilmore has just taken up residence (see page 111).

ROYAL BOTANIC GARDENS

After descending the Monumental Steps at the front of the Opera House, turn left and walk 100 metres to the Queen Elizabeth II Gate, which takes you into the **Royal Botanic Gardens** ➍ (www.rbgsyd.nsw.gov.au; daily 7am–sunset; free). The gardens' 30 hectares (74 acres) loop around Farm Cove, or Woccanmagully ('crow headland'), as Indigenous people call it. The colony's first farm and the gov-ernor's kitchen garden became the Botanic Gardens in 1816. Governor Macquarie appointed Charles Fraser, a soldier, as the first colonial botanist. Explore the gardens by taking the **trackless train** (charge), which tours at regular intervals (with commentary), or simply wandering through.

The harbour islands

Sydney has several harbour islands, some of which are open to visitors. The most notorious is Fort Denison, which gained its nickname 'Pinchgut' from its days as a place of punishment. The island and its small fort are open daily for visitors, and it hosts regular tasting sessions showing off Australian's wine and cheese (www.mcintoshand bowman.com); ferries depart from Circular Quay. Goat Island (open for special events only) – one of the largest – has convict-era architecture and historic port facilities, and is an occasional venue for concerts. Rodd, Clark and Shark islands make great picnic spots and are open every day from 9am to sunset. A regular ferry service runs from the harbour to Shark Island; to visit Clark or Rodd islands, you will need to organise your own transport. For more information on visiting the harbour islands, contact Sydney Harbour National Park Information Centre (tel: 9247 5033; www.nationalparks. nsw.gov.au).

Admiring the displays in the Art Gallery of NSW

Herbs and roses

Start by heading south to the **Herb Garden**, just behind the **Conservatorium of Music** (see page 48), where there are displays charting the history of herbs. In the nearby **Rose Garden**, the plantings demonstrate the history and diversity of the rose. Keep heading south to the magnificent **Tropical Centre**, where you can walk through two modern glasshouses where humidity is kept at a minimum of 75 percent. The **Pyramid** contains native Australian tropical species, while the Arc displays exotic tropicals.

Palm Grove

East of the glasshouses lies **Palm Grove**, which dates to the 19th century and contains nearly 150 species. Nearby is the **RBG Shop and Visitor Centre** (tel: 9231 8125; daily 9.30am–5pm), opposite which lies a stunning **Succulent Garden** featuring cacti and other species from the deserts of South Africa and the Americas.

The Lower Gardens

Keep heading north to the Lower Gardens, 5 hectares (12 acres) of reclaimed turf, landscaped in typical 19th-century style, complete with formal plantings, framed vistas, ornate statues and a series of picturesque little ponds created by the damming of a small creek.

Follow the sea wall heading east and you'll come to the **Fleet Steps**, built for sailors disembarking from ships at Farm Cove. During January and February, the ever-popular St George **Open-Air Cinema** (www.stgeorgeopenair.com.au) is held here, screening new and cult films to late-night picnickers.

Further along is one of Sydney's most popular spots for wedding photos, **Mrs Macquarie's Chair**, a ledge that was carved from sandstone to enable Governor Macquarie's wife to sit comfortably while admiring one of the most magnificent harbour views in the world.

Keep following the foreshore path to come to another of Sydney's waterside swimming pools. The **Andrew (Boy) Charlton Pool** (1c Mrs Macquarie's Road; www.abcpool.org; charge) is named after a swimming champion of the 1920s and 1930s, and has a cafe. The road leads up to The Domain, a 30-hectare (72-acre) spread of open parkland that, during January, hosts free outdoor concerts, featuring a variety of music (including jazz and classical) and opera, which attract up to 100,000 people. Opposite lies the Art Gallery of NSW.

ART GALLERY OF NEW SOUTH WALES (NSW)

Fronted by an imposing 1909 neo-classical facade with a huge portico, the **Art Gallery of NSW ❺** (Art Gallery Road, The Domain; www.artgallery.nsw.gov.au; Thur–Tue 10am–5pm, Wed

The waterfront in Woolloomooloo

10am–9pm; free) is one of the country's best galleries, holding significant collections of Australian, Asian and European art, in addition to hosting special exhibitions, talks and events.

This is a good place to get an overview of Australian art, with artists such as Arthur Boyd, Sidney Nolan, Grace Cossington-Smith, John Olsen and Brett Whiteley all well represented. On the third level, the **Yiribana Gallery** has an outstanding collection of traditional and contemporary Aboriginal and Torres Strait Islander work. Started in the 1950s, it is now one of the largest collections of indigenous art in the world and includes a fine collection of bark paintings.

Also worth visiting is the ground-floor **Asian Gallery**, where artworks from across the region – with particular emphasis on Japanese and Chinese art – are displayed.

WOOLLOOMOOLOO

Leaving the gallery, turn right to find the steps leading down to **Woolloomooloo ❻**. Long one of the city's grittiest areas, and still home to a large amount of public housing, the district's gentrification only started in the 1990s when the 400-metre-long Finger Wharf was redeveloped into apartments, a private marina, a string of stylish waterside restaurants and a hotel. Stop here for some refreshment, or try one of the old-school pubs opposite, such as the

Old Fitzroy Hotel. Alternatively, chow down at the well-loved **Harry's Cafe de Wheels**, see ❷, which has been selling pies since 1945.

Food and drink

❶ OPERA BAR

Lower Concourse Level, Opera House, Bennelong Point; tel: 9247 1666; www.operabar.com.au; Mon–Thur 8am–midnight, Fri 8am–1am, Sat–Sun 9am–1am; $$

The restaurant at Bennelong, the Opera House's fine-dining venue, is an experience, but not one that everyone can afford, so for those looking for a great Sydney experience at a cheaper price, the indoor-outdoor Opera Bar is the place to go. During the day, the vibe is relaxed; at night, it is positively buzzing, with DJs spinning great tunes.

❷ HARRY'S CAFE DE WHEELS

Cowper Wharf Road, Woolloomooloo; tel: 9211 2506; www.harryscafedewheels. com.au; Mon–Tues 8.30am–2am, Weds–Thurs 8.30am–3am, Fri 8.30am–4am, Sat 9am–4am, Sun 9am–1am; $

Harry's is a Sydney institution. For over 60 years, a peas-and-mash pie (now called 'The Tiger') has been the favourite way to finish up a big night. Even during the day you will often see punters queuing to sink their teeth into one of Harry's finest.

St Mary's Cathedral

THE CBD AND WALSH BAY

This tour is one for architecture buffs, taking in the highlights of the Central Business District (CBD), where Sydney's mini–Manhattan skyline is studded with statement buildings by internationally acclaimed architects, punctuated with older gems from the colonial and Victorian periods. Nearby is Walsh Bay.

DISTANCE: 7km (4.5 miles)
TIME: A half-day
START: St Mary's Cathedral
END: 30 The Bond
POINTS TO NOTE: St Mary's Cathedral is located on the eastern side of Hyde Park. Start this tour in the afternoon and aim to finish in the evening, when the theatre district comes alive and you can savour a glass of wine and a snack in one of the area's waterside bars.

Two hundred years of history are revealed in the streetscapes of Sydney's Central Business District (CBD), where the ongoing battle between preservation and progress has resulted in buildings from different decades and different centuries nestling cheek by jowl.

An architectural history
The city's most homogeneous architectural zones are the adjoining areas of Macquarie Street and Martin Place, which serve as an interesting illustration of the colony's changing ambitions. The early government buildings lining Macquarie Street are relatively modest sandstone constructions; less than a century later, a growing self-confidence led to the far more grandiose Victorian visions planted on Martin Place by capitalists grown rich on exporting commodities such as wool.

Although the building boom of the 1960s and 1970s destroyed many of the city's historic buildings, a lot of the survivors – such as Customs House and the former GPO – have been restored recently. For the past 30 years, Sydney's skyline has been dominated by an urban obelisk formerly known as Centrepoint Tower, but now called the Sydney Tower Eye. At 303 metres (990ft) it's still the city's highest structure. As late as the 1960s, that honour was held by the AMP building at Circular Quay, which is now dwarfed by all its neighbours. And the city's silhouette continues to evolve, most recently with new buildings by internationally

The CBD by night

Historic architecture in central Sydney

acclaimed architects such as Renzo Piano, and industrial conversions such as the wharves along Hickson Road. Two buildings over 200 metres tall are currently in construction – the Greenland Centre in the CBD, and the International Towers in Barangaroo near Millers Point – with another seven proposed to be built 2020.

ST MARY'S CATHEDRAL

The city's most significant Catholic cathedral and one of Sydney's most impressive Victorian structures, **St Mary's Cathedral ❶** (corner of College and Cathedral streets; www.stmaryscathedral.org.au; Mon–Fri 7am–6pm, Sat 8.30am–7pm, Sun 7am–7pm; charge for crypt only) was designed by an Anglican, William Wardell, in Gothic style. The vaulted roof reaches 46 metres (150ft) into the heavens. The cathedral opened in 1885, but due to money issues, the twin spires – part of the original design – were only completed in the 1990s, when they were lowered on by helicopter. The highlight of the magnificent interior is the gorgeous terrazzo floor of the crypt, inlaid with Celtic patterns and an illustration of the six days of creation. To enter, buy a ticket from the cathedral shop, near the College Street entrance.

HYDE PARK BARRACKS

Follow Prince Albert Road north to the traffic lights and continue into Mac-

Exterior of Hyde Park Barracks

quarie Street, the closest thing Sydney has to a grand boulevard. In the colony's early days, this was the administrative quarter; today, Sydney's top medical specialists operate from offices in a series of beautiful Art Deco edifices.

The building on the corner with College Street is **Hyde Park Barracks** ❷ (Queens Square, Macquarie Street; www.sydneylivingmuseums.com.au/hyde-park-barracks-museum; daily 9.30am–5pm; charge). This was the first proper jail in Australia, opened in 1819, 30 years after the colony's founding. As a penal settlement, Sydney had a population that consisted mainly of convicts, but jails were not seen as a huge priority because the harsh environment and climate meant would-be escapees had nowhere to run. Ironically, Hyde Park Barracks was designed by a former convict. Francis Greenway had been sentenced to 14 years' transportation for forgery in 1814, but his design talents were soon recognised by Governor Macquarie, who enlisted him in his building campaign to transform the face of Sydney. Greenway's architectural legacy was so strong that for many years the ex-con's portrait appeared on Australia's $10 note.

Hyde Park Barracks served as a jail for 30 years, and thereafter as a female immigration depot, an asylum for the aged and infirm, a court and as government buildings. Now the barracks house a changing series of exhibitions dedicated to convict life and the building's history.

RUM HOSPITAL

Greenway also designed the next three sights: the Mint, Sydney Hospital and Parliament House, which once formed a huge edifice housing Sydney's first hospital. Known as the Rum Hospital, its story reveals a lot about the way the colony was run in its early days. Three merchants agreed to fund the hospital in return for a monopoly on the importation of rum, the rowdy colony's most precious currency at the time. The original building was so shoddily constructed that the main body (now Sydney Hospital) had to be rebuilt under Greenway's direction. The hospital's two wings were eventually requisitioned to serve as the Mint and Parliament House. Both wings have undergone considerable renovation, but still retain features dating to the original 1811 building.

Parliament House

There is something very laidback about New South Wales' **Parliament House** ❸ (Macquarie Street; www.parliament.nsw.gov.au; Mon–Fri 9am–5pm; free). With its double verandas, pastel-coloured awnings and decorative ironwork, it looks like it belongs in Queensland. The interior feels slightly more formal, taking as its inspiration the interiors of London's Houses of Parliament, right down to the colour scheme (red for the upper chamber, green for the lower).

Tours are available at different times, depending on whether Parliament is sit-

Inside the barracks   *Office buildings in the CBD*

ting – see the website for more details. It is also possible to watch proceedings from the public galleries when Parliament is sitting.

MARTIN PLACE

Situated directly opposite Sydney Hospital lies Martin Place, the largest open space in the CBD, which was the scene of a dramatic siege in December 2014, when a lone gunman held 18 people hostage in the Lindt cafe for 16 hours, before a shootout resulted in three deaths. The incident was believed to be a terrorist attack as it unfolded on world screens, but this has since been debated. A memorial to the victims is planned.

The southern side of the plaza is lined with fine Victorian sandstone buildings erected with the profits of booming wheat and wool industries. One of the most striking is the Commonwealth Bank building between Castlereagh and Elizabeth streets, one of several buildings that the bank owns along the plaza. Finished in 1928, the neoclassical building has a magnificent interior, including a two-storey marble-banking chamber that is visible through the building's windows.

GPO Sydney

You will need to walk all the way down to George Street to see Martin Place's most magnificent monument, but it is well worth the detour. The former General Post Office, known these days as the **GPO Grand** ❹ (1 Martin Place; www.gpogrand.com; daily, hours differ according to venue; free) was designed by James Barnet, who was responsible for many of 19th-century Sydney's most elegant buildings. These days, the GPO houses several acclaimed restaurants and bars, including Prime Restaurant and Postales. Even if you're not hungry, take a walk inside to admire the magnificently restored interior, complete with ornately decorated staircases.

AURORA PLACE

Walk back up Martin Place and turn left when you reach Elizabeth Street. After about 300 metres you will come to the intersection with Hunter Street. On your right rises one of Sydney's newest landmarks, **Aurora Place** ❺. Walk one block north to reach it, at the junction of Philip Street and Bent Street. Designed by acclaimed Italian architect Renzo Piano, it consists of two buildings: a slender 18-storey apartment block and a 41-storey office tower. The glass curtain-wall seems to float independently, while the curves pay homage to the Opera House.

MUSEUM OF SYDNEY

Head north, and at the next intersection (with Bridge Street) you'll find the **Museum of Sydney** ❻ (corner of Bridge and Phillip streets; www.sydneyliving museums.com.au/museum-of-sydney; daily 9.30am–5pm; charge), located on the site of the colony's first Government

Government House

House. As you walk through the 29 pillars (representing the 29 local clans) of the *Edge of the Trees* sculpture at the main entrance, you'll hear place names from around Sydney spoken in the Eora languages of the area's original Aboriginal inhabitants.

The Museum of Sydney has a variety of changing exhibitions, as well as permanent displays commemorating the 'Sydney Visionaries' who shaped the city, and a gallery dedicated to the local Cadigal people. The stories of individuals such as Patyegarang, Barangaro and Colebee – the last a tribal chief who was at first imprisoned, but escaped and later used to dine with Captain Phillip of the First Fleet – are a reminder of how fluid and complex relationships between black and white were in the early days of the colony. The museum's sleek eating-house, the **Governors Table**, see ①, is a popular spot.

CONSERVATORIUM OF MUSIC

From the museum, head up Bridge Street to Macquarie Street. On the opposite side of the road you will see the **Conservatorium of Music** (www.music.sydney.edu.au), which has just celebrated its centenary. The original building – on the left, with crenelated towers – was designed by Francis Greenway to serve as the stables for Government House. Together with the adjoining modern extension, it now houses the city's most talented musical students. Staff and students often perform concerts in the new building, and admission fees are modest.

GOVERNMENT HOUSE

Trace the Conservatorium's driveway left into the Royal Botanic Gardens and follow the sign to **Government House** ❼ (Macquarie Street; www.sydneyliving museums.com.au/government-house; grounds daily 10am–4pm, house open for tours only, Fri–Sun 10.30am–3pm every half-hour; free). Designed by the English architect Edward Blore, who was also involved in the creation of Buckingham Palace in London, this frivolous Romantic mock castle built between 1837 and 1845 is as absurdly out of place as it is charming.

Government House remained the residence of the State Governor until the mid-1990s, when the Labor premier snatched this perk of office away from the incumbent and opened it to the people instead, introducing a programme of cultural events including concerts. The house contains impressive collections of colonial furniture and paintings, as well as contemporary works by NSW artists, craftspeople and designers. A stroll through the historic gardens is recommended.

CUSTOMS HOUSE

Exiting the gates of Government House, go north along the service road; this will bring you to another set of gates on to Macquarie Street. Directly across the

Museum of Sydney

road is a set of stairs leading down to the harbour. Take the stairs and turn left at the bottom, following the water around to Circular Quay. Walk along Circular Quay until you reach Wharf 4, opposite which stands another of James Barnet's gems, **Customs House** ❽ (31 Alfred Street; www.sydneycustoms house.com.au; Mon–Fri 10am–7pm, Sat–Sun 11am–4pm; free).

Dating from 1885, this building is reputed to stand on the site where the Union flag was first flown in Sydney. The building's award-winning interiors now contain a full-scale model of the CBD under the floor of the atrium, and there are various multimedia facilities, as well as free wireless internet. There are bars and restaurants here too, including the Quay Bar and Cafe Sydney.

WALSH BAY

Exiting Customs House, turn left and walk up Alfred Street towards George Street. If you are in need of refreshment, you can stop in at **Fred's Bar and Bistro**, see ❷, or **Cruise Restaurant**, see ❸; alternatively, turn right into George Street then left at the next intersection. Walk up Argyle Street through the convict-chiselled tunnel called the Argyle Cut, past Observatory Hill on your left and the Garrison Church on your right. Turn right into Kent Street and after a block you'll come to Windmill Steps, which descend into Walsh Bay (www. walshbaysydney.com.au).

Turn right and walk along the wharves to **The Wharf Theatre** ❾ (Pier 4–5 Hickson Road; www.sydneytheatre. com.au; daily; free), the original home of the **Sydney Theatre Company** (STC). Even if you are not catching a performance, sneak upstairs and walk the atmospheric corridor, lined with massive timber beams, to where The Wharf restaurant enjoys a magnificent water view.

On the other side of the road is the STC's newer venue, **Sydney Theatre** – also worth a peek. The theatre occupies a former Bond Stores (warehouse), and the design has kept the old distressed walls, as well as recycling original timbers to stunning effect.

The wharves opposite the Sydney Theatre have been redeveloped to cater for Sydney's insatiable hunger for luxury waterfront living. The complexes host several pleasant wine bars and restaurants, most notably **Ventuno**, see ❹.

30 The Bond

Head south along Hickson Road, veering left at the lights, for about 600 metres. On the left is **30 The Bond** ❿, headquarters of property group LendLease – the first office block in central Sydney to achieve a five-star energy rating, and one of the city's most impressive modern buildings. The external stairs seem to float, while the back wall of the atrium is a four-storey convict-hewn sandstone wall (take a look through the building's glass walls near the stairs).

This whole area will soon have some

Cultural pursuits.

new giant shadows, however, as a trio of cloud-scraping business buildings called the International Towers continue their climb into the sky above a mini-suburb that is now being called Barangaroo South (www.barangaroosouth.com.au). Eye-pleasing parks and water features have been promised by developers, so watch this space.

From here, return to the city centre by taking the stairs or the lift to the top of the plateau. Head right and then left into Gas Lane, which will bring you up to Kent Street. Cross the road and follow the path south to Clarence Street. At the second set of lights, turn left into Margaret Street and walk two blocks up to George Street. Three blocks west is Wynyard station.

Food and drink

① THE GOVERNORS TABLE

Corner of Bridge and Phillip streets; tel: 9241 1788; www.thegovernorstable.com.au; Mon 7.30am–5pm, Tue–Fri 7.30am–late, Sat 8.30am–late, Sun 9.30am–5pm; $

Classy food in a classy setting, quietly influenced by its cerebral surrounds, from the use of materials mirroring *The Edge of the Trees* indigenous installation in the museum's forecourt, through to subtle Scandinavian touches in the interior design.

② FRED'S BAR AND BISTRO

1 Alfred St; tel: 9251 0384; www.fredsbar. com.au; Mon–Fri 7.30am–late; $$

Propping up iconic Goldfields House in a perfect position on Circular Quay, Fred's caters for travellers and local business types looking for good food complimented by a drop of something special. Internationally experienced hosts David Moeliker and Erica Gregan know how to mix quality with comfort. Offerings range from classic fish and chips through to Salad

Nicoise and Fred's Charcuterie Selection. Open from breakfast onwards, but shut all weekend.

③ CRUISE RESTAURANT

Level 2, Overseas Passenger Terminal; tel: 9119 1849; www.cruisebar.com.au; Sun–Thur 11am–Midnight, Fri–Sat 11am–1am; $$–$$$$

Watch the world arrive and depart from the Terrace Bar or the Junk Lounge while you munch. With prime views of the Opera House and the harbour, it is no surprise that the chic restaurants in the Overseas Passenger Terminal will never make a cheap-eats list. Cruise remains a favourite, its sophisticated food a match for the splendid view.

④ VENTUNO

21 Hickson Road; tel: 9247 4444; www.ventuno.com.au; daily noon–late; $–$$

This stylish yet relaxed eatery specialises in pizza, but also offers a broad array of pasta and meat dishes. Its indoor-outdoor setting makes it the perfect place to while away a balmy night or a lazy Sunday afternoon.

Admiring the sharks through transparent underwater tunnels at the aquarium

DARLING HARBOUR

For years a derelict harbourside neighbourhood, Darling Harbour is now one of the city's most visited areas. From family friendly attractions to bars, museums and even a casino, it has more than enough to fill a day.

DISTANCE: 4.25km (2.6 miles)
TIME: A full day
START: Sydney Aquarium
END: Pyrmont Bridge
POINTS TO NOTE: You can reach the Aquarium either by walking west down Market Street, or catching the monorail to Darling Park. If you do this route in the week, attractions such as the Aquarium and the Chinese Garden will be less busy; at weekends, the crowds are larger, but the street entertainers will be out.

Hidden behind the city's skyscrapers, the Darling Harbour precinct has reinvented itself several times over the last 20 years. During the first stage, Darling Harbour itself, was redeveloped as a family focussed destination in time for the bicentennial in 1988. Since then, it has been joined by two cityside precincts, Cockle Bay and King Street wharves, which feature a number of popular restaurants and bars. This route takes in the highlights of all three, as well as the surrounding area.

This relatively compact area is easy to negotiate on foot, but a monorail loops around Darling Harbour (travelling anticlockwise only), and the Light Rail service that runs from Central Railway along the western edge of Darling Harbour is useful for getting to the Powerhouse.

SYDNEY AQUARIUM

Australia is an island continent, and the **Sydney Aquarium** ❶ (Aquarium Pier, Darling Harbour; tel: 133 FUN; www.sydney aquarium.com.au; daily 9am–8pm; charge) showcases the astonishing creatures that inhabit the waters around the continent, and also around the world.

Begin by inspecting the 50 tanks that hold around 5,000 sea creatures, from blue starfish the size of a dinner plate to saltwater crocodiles. The main attractions, however, are the two floating oceanariums. One is home to dugongs, a marine mammal found in the warmer waters of northern Australia; the other contains a vast number of sharks and giant rays, which are viewed from transparent underwater tunnels. There can

Wallabies at Wildlife World

be long queues for the oceanariums, but they are worth it: the sight of these enormous creatures floating by just metres away is not one you'll forget in a hurry.

WILDLIFE WORLD

Once you surface from your underwater explorations, it's off to meet the terrestrial delights of **Wildlife World** ❷ (Aquarium Pier, Darling Harbour; tel: 133 FUN; www.sydneywildlifeworld. com.au; daily 9am–5pm; charge), right next door. Australia's many weird and wonderful species are on display here, from venomous spiders to an astonishing array of reptiles; the continent has 840 reptile species, com-

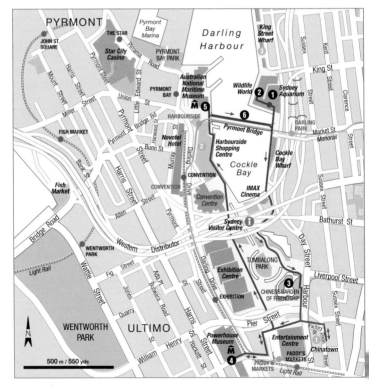

The Chinese Garden

pared with just 280 in North America. Australia also has the most poisonous species of snakes in the world.

There is also a collection of nocturnal animals, this being the only continent to have more animals active in the night than during the day. As well as special koala and kangaroo enclosures, there are nine unique Australian habitats, from wallaby-filled grasslands to the tropical rainforest where you can walk around surrounded by thousands of colourful butterflies. From ghost bats and bilbies to wombats and cassowaries, this place has them all.

CHINESE GARDEN

From here, follow the water's edge south, heading inland past the IMAX 3-D cinema and the old-fashioned carousel, to the children's play area. Veer left and follow the signs for the **Chinese Garden of Friendship** ❸ (daily 9.30am–5pm; charge).

A bicentennial gift from the government of China's Guangdong province, the garden is an enchanting confection of ponds clad with water lilies, picturesque wooden bridges and plants, including four types of bamboo, evergreen pines and willows, the flowering apricot and red silk cotton trees (the floral emblem of Guangdong).

End your visit with tea in the traditional teahouse, a peaceful respite before heading onwards.

CHINATOWN

Continue south, following the signs to the Entertainment Centre. Cross Harbour Street and walk up Factory Street to reach Dixon Street, the heart of Sydney's Chinatown. The Chinese have been coming to Australia since 1818, with spikes in arrivals during the 1850s Gold Rush, and the 1990s and early 21st century. According to the last census, 7 percent of Sydneysiders have a Chinese heritage, and the city's China Town is a vibrant place to explore. If you're hungry, there are countless eateries to choose from here, including **Superbowl**, see ①. The food court on the corner of Dixon and Factory streets also offers cheap-and-cheerful meals.

POWERHOUSE MUSEUM

Now head back to the Entertainment Centre and, skirting its northern side, walk past the car park until you come to the steps leading up to the footbridge next to Paddy's Market monorail. Walk across to the western side, turn left and you'll reach the sprawling **Powerhouse Museum** ❹ (500 Harris Street Ultimo; daily 10am–5pm, www.maas.museum/powerhouse-museum; charge), one of Australia's best museums.

Its brief covers science, technology, decorative arts and popular culture; over the years, it has featured exhibits on topics from Kylie Minogue's stage costumes to artificial intelligence and

Evidence of Australia's naval history at the Maritime Museum

the history of housework. The interactive approach makes it fun for families. The permanent exhibitions alone could easily take half a day to explore.

The museum's Space exhibition features everything from rocket motors to shuttle tiles, spacesuits and a moon rock. The highlight is a **Zero Gravity Space Lab** that creates the illusion of being in a weightless environment. The Transport gallery on Level 1 covers more conventional vehicles, from hansom cabs and vintage motorcycles to various kinds of aeroplane. The first train ever used in Australia, Locomotive Number One, is displayed on Level 3.

EcoLogic, an exhibit devoted to sustainability, highlights the changes we can make to our lifestyles and industries to protect the environment. The **Success and Innovations** exhibit looks at some of Australia's most successful industrial designs, from Victa lawnmowers to the world's first animated superstar, Felix the Cat. Kids will love the hands-on exhibits, including one that lets them try their hand at shearing an electronic sheep.

Another favourite with children is the **Experimentations** section, which has more than 30 interactive exhibits that demonstrate the principles of temperature and pressure, electricity and magnetism, light, gravity and motion, and chemistry.

The **Chemical Attractions** section, which looks at how chemicals are used in everyday products to stimulate our senses, is also popular – predictably, the chocolate exhibit is particularly so.

The museum's most valuable exhibit – part of its display dedicated to the steam revolution – is the Boulton and Watt steam engine, the oldest surviving rotational steam engine in the world. The museum also has play areas for younger children, and a courtyard cafe that's a great place to take a break.

AUSTRALIAN NATIONAL MARITIME MUSEUM

Leaving the museum, retrace your route along the footbridge. At the bottom of the stairs, head north through the heart of **Darling Harbour** (www.darlingharbour.com), past Tumbalong Park and the Convention Centre, and through **Harbourside Shopping Centre** (www.harbourside.com.au; daily 10am–9pm, restaurants open later). This is a good stop for lunch, consider picking up a pizza at **Criniti's**, see ❷. Carry on and you'll see the unmistakable **Australian National Maritime Museum ❺** (2 Murray Street, Darling Harbour; www.anmm.gov.au; daily 9.30am–5pm; charge), which has a modern destroyer (HMAS *Vampire*), a submarine (HMAS *Onslow*) and a recreation of Captain Cook's Endeavour all parked out the front. Access to all of these vessels is included in the ticket price. Inside, exhibits are grouped thematically in categories such as discovery, commerce, defence and leisure. The most moving exhibi-

Darling Harbour at night

tion, about human migration, traces the voyages of convicts, free settlers, post-World War II European immigrants and refugees from the Vietnam War.

A range of working vessels is exhibited both inside and outside the museum, from a Vietnamese fishing boat to the *Australia II* yacht, which won the 1983 America's Cup and created a wave of national jubilation.

PYRMONT BRIDGE

Head back to Cockle Bay Wharf via **Pyrmont Bridge** ❻. The first bridge built here was a private toll one; pedestrians paid tuppence each way, while sheep and pigs were charged a farthing a head. The current structure was considered a masterpiece of modern engineering when it opened in 1902, with an 800-tonne, 70-metre (230ft) electronic 'swing span' that pivots horizontally to let large vessels enter the inner harbour.

Finish off the walk by heading north along the water to King Street Wharf, where you can relax in one of the area's many bars and restaurants, such as **The Loft**, see ❸.

Food and drink

❶ SUPERBOWL

41 Dixon Street, Chinatown; tel: 9281 2462; daily 8am–2am; $–$$

A great example of the no-frills dining that Chinatown does so well. There is plenty of Cantonese seafood and barbecue on offer, as well as provincial specials such as shredded jellyfish. The house speciality is congee, a savoury rice porridge.

❷ CRINITIS DARLING HARBOUR

Level 2, Harbourside Shopping Centre; tel: 1300 274 648; www.crinitis.com. au; Sun–Thur 8am–10.30pm, Fri–Sat 8am–11.30pm; $–$$

Location, location, location. All of Darling Harbour lies below you from a seat on the terrace. And food, food, food. Possibly the best pizzas in Sydney, including the infamous Pizza al Metro, a 1-metre pizza served hot on a long wooden board.

❸ THE LOFT

3 Lime Street, King Street Wharf; tel: 8070 2424; www.theloftsydney.com.au; Mon–Fri 4pm–late, Sat noon–3am, Sun noon–1am; $$

Luscious leather sofas, floral fretwork on the ceilings and walls and geometric cut-out screens in rich burnt colours give The Loft a 21st-century Moroccan feel. A sophisticated young crowd indulges in tapas, such as the Asian platter (tempura prawns, sticky Mongolian pork ribs, sushi) or the South American platter (spicy empanadas, chilli- and chocolate-glazed pork strips), and cocktails.

Ibis at Elizabeth Bay House

ELIZABETH BAY TO SURRY HILLS

A walk through Sydney's trendy inner-city suburbs is a study in contrasts. From graceful 19th-century architecture to hip bars and cafes, pocket-sized boutiques to world-class dining – it offers a slice of real Sydney life.

DISTANCE: 5km (3 miles)
TIME: A half-day
START: Elizabeth Bay House
END: Crown Street
POINTS TO NOTE: To reach Elizabeth Bay House, take bus No. 311 from the city (see www.131500.info), and ask to be let out at the closest stop. This route has two endings, depending on how far you feel like walking. In either case, start the tour in the afternoon, and you will be able to finish with a drink in one of the city's hip bars, either in Darlinghurst or Surry Hills. If you want to take in the Brett Whiteley studio (see page 60), do the route on a weekend. The shorter version of this route can be combined with route 6 (see page 62).

There are few monuments or museums in Sydney's inner suburbs, but a couple of hours spent wandering the streets of Potts Point, Kings Cross, Darlinghurst and Surry Hills offers one of the best insights into Sydney's vibrant and diverse heart. The sleaze of the Kings Cross strip blends into chic Potts Point at one end and hip Darlinghurst at the other, while the backstreets of 'the Cross' house some of the city's most elegant residential architecture. Some of the main sights along the way are indicated, but the real joy of this walk is soaking up the inner-city vibe, stopping off at whichever cafes, boutiques or galleries catch your eye.

ELIZABETH BAY HOUSE

The grandest house in town when it was built in 1839, **Elizabeth Bay House** ❶ (7 Onslow Avenue, Elizabeth Bay; www.sydneylivingmuseums.com.au/elizabeth-bay-house; Fri–Sun 9.30am–4pm; charge) gives a sense of how the colony's elite used to live. The design is attributed to John Verge, but the original owner, Colonial Secretary Alexander Macleay, drove down every day during the four-year construction period to supervise the work personally. The house's most magnificent feature is an elliptical saloon dominated by a

Elizabeth Bay House

Sitting by the dandelion-shaped El Alamein Fountain

curving cantilevered staircase under a dome. Macleay was only able to enjoy the house for a few years before his son, from whom he'd borrowed much of the money to finance the house, took occupancy, sending his father to live with his sister.

Elizabeth Bay House was once famous for its 22 hectares (54 acres) of gardens, which included orchards, flower gardens, a kitchen garden and a vast collection of native and exotic plants. Most of the gardens are now covered by apartment blocks; the pocket park opposite the house itself, with its pretty grotto, is one of the few visible remnants.

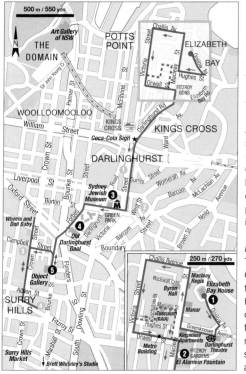

TOWARDS POTTS POINT

On leaving Elizabeth Bay House, turn right into Onslow Avenue and follow the road for around 100 metres up to the intersection with Elizabeth Bay Road and Greenknowe Avenue. Near the intersection with Onslow Avenue, on the south side of Greenknowe Avenue, is **Darlinghurst Theatre**, one of the city's premier performance venues for independent drama.

Macleay Street

Turn right and head up Greenknowe Avenue to Macleay Street, the heart of the chic enclave of **Potts Point**, known for its lively cafes and restaurants as well as some of the city's most attractive residential

architecture. The layout is no happy accident – even in the 1830s, Potts Point, then known as Woolloomooloo Hill, was subject to planning controls. Anyone who received a land grant in the area had conditions imposed on their houses, including the budget (at least £1,000), the orientation (facing the city) and an approvals process (the Governor had to give the design the thumbs up).

Just before the intersection with Macleay are the ornate **Kingsclere Apartments**, one of the first high-rise apartment blocks of flats in Sydney. Built in 1912, the exclusive apartments each had two balconies and two bathrooms, wood panelling and automatic passenger lifts.

As you head north along Macleay Street, you will see more grand apartment buildings from the 1920s and 1930s, including the **Macleay Regis** at No. 122, **Byron Hall** at No. 97–9, and **Manar** at No. 42.

Victoria Street

Turn left into Challis Avenue then, at the end of the street, left into Victoria Street. The grand Greek Revival houses in Challis Avenue and the imposing terraces on Victoria Street in this inner-city suburb of Potts Point were threatened by developers in the 1960s and 1970s. Like the old houses in The Rocks (see page 30), they were saved from developers by the 'green bans', imposed by the Builders' Labourers Federation. Their members supported the protests of the local community by refusing to work on the threatened sites. Among the prominent local supporters of the green bans was heiress Juanita Nielsen, who lived at 202 Victoria Street. As proprietor of a local newspaper, she fought against the developers, which is widely assumed to be the reason for her disappearance, and presumed murder, in July 1975.

Walk along the plane tree–lined Victoria Street for about 200 metres, before turning left up either Hughes or Orwell Street. Orwell Street is home to Art Deco buildings including the curving **Metro Building** on your left, where the Australian premiere of the musical Hair provoked outrage in the 1960s.

Alternatively, head up Hughes Street and turn left into Tusculum Street, then right into Manning Street, to admire the elegant facade of **Tusculum**, another of the mansions Verge designed for the area. Today Tusculum is home to the Royal Australian Institute of Architects (RAIA).

KINGS CROSS

Both Hughes and Orwell streets lead back to Macleay Street. Head south past the city's most distinctive fountain, the dandelion-shaped **El Alamein Fountain ❷**, which marks the division between genteel Potts Point and the more raucous Kings Cross, and com-

Welcome to 'the Cross'

memorates the soldiers who died during the two battles at El Alamein in Egypt during World War II.

Follow Darlinghurst Road up to Kings Cross itself, which straddles the intersection of five streets dominated by a massive neon Coca-Cola sign. Often claimed to be the largest lit-up billboard in the southern hemisphere, the Kings Cross Coca-Cola sign measures 41 metres in length by 13 metres in height, and it's been providing business for Sydney's dentists since 1974.

A history of vice

Originally as upmarket as the neighbouring areas, 'the Cross', as this 'hood is commonly known, developed a bohemian reputation in the 1930s and 1940s, attracting poets and painters such as Mary Gilmore and William Dobell. Artist Donald Friend reminisced about the 'genuine Berlin air' of the Cross in the 1940s, describing it as a place where 'everybody is wicked'. The area's proximity to the Garden Island naval base and the Woolloomooloo docks made it a popular recreation spot for servicemen during World War II and the Vietnam War, leading to the introduction of the seedy strip clubs that, along with backpacker hostels, now characterise the main drag.

A series of plaques on the footpath commemorates the area's history, including the first gay protest march in 1978 that evolved into the annual Gay Mardi Gras parade.

DARLINGHURST

Continue straight across the Cross and, when Darlinghurst Road splits into two, take the left-hand fork, Victoria Street, which from here to Liverpool Street is packed with boutiques and cafes, including **Tropicana Caffe**, see ❶, and, a few blocks down Liverpool Street, **Bill's**, see ❷.

From Victoria Street, turn right into Burton Street and walk up a block. On the corner with Darlinghurst Road is the **Sydney Jewish Museum** ❸ (148 Darlinghurst Road; www.sydneyjewish museum.com.au; Mon–Thur 10am–4pm, Fri 10am–2pm, Sun 10am–4pm; charge). The main exhibits focus on the Holocaust, but part of the museum is devoted to the history of Jewish life in Australia, from the arrival of the First Fleet – which carried 16 Jewish convicts – to the present day; there is also a kosher cafe.

Darlinghurst Gaol

The magnificent collection of sandstone buildings on the block bounded by Darlinghurst, Burton and Forbes streets is the **Old Darlinghurst Gaol** ❹. Today it is home to the National Art School, and closed to the public, but looking through the gates on Burton Street will give you a sense of the scale of the place.

Begun in 1822, the first cellblocks were completed in 1840, and the first inmates moved in the following year. Construction continued around them

Darlinghurst Gaol

until the gaol was completed in 1885. Seventy-nine people were hanged at Darlinghurst Gaol, the last in 1907. Crowds would gather at nearby Green Park to view the hangings, which took place on a platform high enough to be visible above the prison's high walls.

SURRY HILLS

You can either finish your walk here, with a drink in one of the venues on Victoria Street or Darlinghurst Road, or walk south a little further down Forbes Street to reach Oxford Street, one of Sydney's most famous thoroughfares. For years, the lower end of Oxford Street was Sydney's gay golden mile, while the upper end constituted one of Sydney's most exclusive shopping precincts. The lower end is now a bit tawdry, but the side streets of Surry Hills offer plenty of opportunities for shopping, eating and browsing.

If you're here on the first Saturday of the month, be sure to check out Surry Hills Market – a great community affair where the emphasis is on a range of pre-loved and handmade goods; you'll find it around the Shannon Reserve on the corner of Crown and Collins streets.

St Margarets Complex
At the lights, cross and walk south down Bourke Street about 100 metres to **St Margarets Complex**, a former hospital that is now home to the **Object Gallery ❺** (417 Bourke Street, Surry Hills; www.object.com.au; Tue–Fri 11am–5pm, Sat–Sun 10am–5pm; free). The gallery features the best of Australian craft and design, and is housed in a chapel formerly used by nuns.

Crown Street
To continue, head north back along Bourke Street and go west at Campbell Street to reach Crown Street, which is home to an ever-changing

Brett Whiteley's Studio

There is something so reflective of Sydney about Brett Whiteley's work, from the dazzling blue harbourscapes (seen in Opera House, see page 40) to the whimsical yet philosophical matchsticks sculpture outside the Art Gallery of NSW (see page 42). One of the most talented Australian artists to emerge in the early 1960s, Whiteley struggled with heroin addiction for 20 years before dying in 1992, aged just 53; some of his inner turmoil was reflected in his work. His studio (2 Raper Street, Surry Hills; www.brettwhiteley.org; Sat–Sun 10am–4pm; free) features changing exhibitions, and curious collections of objects are arranged as displays in themselves. It is accessible from this route; from Bourke Street, turn right into Davies, then Raper Street is the second on your left.

Crown Street fashion

Commemorative plaque in Kings Cross

roster of boutiques, restaurants and cafes; for a healthy option, try **Madam Char Chars**, see ③.

Head north to find boutiques such as **Wheels and Doll Baby** at 259 Crown Street, which has been delivering rock-chick chic for years. The label has now gone global, but this is the store where it all started.

Alternatively, for some of Sydney's best eating and drinking options, head south along Crown Street to find Sydney foodies' favourites such as **Marque**, see ④, with chef Mark Best bowling critics and diners over with his modern Aussie tucker. When you are ready, return to Oxford Street to catch a bus heading back to town.

Food and drink

① TROPICANA CAFFE

227 Victoria Street, Darlinghurst; tel: 9360 9809; www.tropicanacaffe.com; daily 5am–11pm; $

There is nothing flash about this local favourite, but it is still the place to stop for a coffee or a hearty salad. The world's largest short film festival, Tropfest, held every February, is named after the cafe, where it was first held.

② BILL'S

433 Liverpool Street, Darlinghurst; tel: 9360 9631; www.bills.com.au; Mon–Sat 7.30am–3pm, Sun 8am–3pm; $–$$

Chef Bill Granger owes his fame to his cookbooks and television appearances. His oldest Sydney outlet (there are three) is on this sunny corner terrace. It serves one of Sydney's best brunches: ricotta hotcakes with fresh banana and honeycomb butter, and sweetcorn fritters with roast tomato, spinach and bacon.

③ MADAM CHAR CHAR

285A Crown Street; 9380 4411; www.madamcharchar.com.au; Mon–Fri 11am–9pm, Sat–Sun 11am–8.30pm; $

Super juicy slow-cooked rotisserie chickens and gourmet burgers, served with all sorts of healthy but hearty salads, marinades that include a secret nan's relish – this is fast food without the coronary side effects. Chill out in the street-facing bar and watch Crown Street pass you by.

④ MARQUE RESTAURANT

4/5 355 Crown Street; tel: 9332 2225; www.marquerestaurant.com.au; Mon–Thur Fri 6.30pm–late, Fri noon–late, Sat 6pm–late; $$$

Former electrician turned master chef Mark Best has lit Crown Street up with Marque, getting rave reviews ('a symbol of New Australian cuisine') all over the place with his signature dishes. Can't choose? Splash on the 8-course degustation menu paired with wines.

The area attracts a young fashionable crowd

PADDINGTON AND WOOLLAHRA

These two upmarket neighbourhoods are ground zero for Sydney's fashion and art scenes. Check out global fashion names, as well as the next big thing at Paddington Markets.

DISTANCE: 8km (5 miles)
TIME: A full day
START: Victoria Barracks
END: Woollahra
POINTS TO NOTE: From the city, catch a bus going to Oxford Street and ask to be let off at the Victoria Barracks stop. The route is best done on a Saturday in order to visit Paddington Markets; allow a couple of hours to see the markets in full, if possible.

Once a slum, Paddington is now one of Sydney's most glittering neighbourhoods. Oxford Street is the city's golden mile for shopping, while the suburb's backstreets are lined with terraces, trees and charming boutiques and galleries. Yet like much of Sydney, Paddington's early history is dominated by the military.

VICTORIA BARRACKS

Victoria Barracks ❶ (corner of Oxford Street and Greens Road; tel: 8335 5170; Thur tour 10am; museum 10am–3pm; free), were built to replace the existing barracks near Wynyard station. The site was chosen because it was accessible to both the harbour and Botany Bay. Work began in 1841 and was due to be completed in two and a half years; ultimately, it took three times as long. The Barracks, still a working site, house a museum that will appeal to those with a bent for uniforms, guns and medals. The guards on duty wear traditional colonial uniforms. Many of the cottages built to house the convict workforce can still be seen in the streets running off Oxford Street, opposite the barracks – such as Bourke Lane and Shadforth Street.

GLENMORE ROAD

Heading east on Oxford Street, the second street on your left is **Glenmore Road ❷**. This was Paddington's first major road, created by bullock carts hauling gin to Oxford Street from Glenmore Distillery near Rushcutters Bay. Today the stretch of Glenmore Road adjoining Oxford Street is home to art galleries and some of Sydney's most stylish clothing shops.

Paddington boutique   *Strolling through Paddington*

Chic boutiques

Fashionistas will want to check out designers such as **Kirrily Johnston** at No. 6 (tel: 9380 7775; www.kirrilyjohnston.com; Mon–Sat 10am–6pm, Sun 11am–5pm); **Ginger and Smart** at No. 16a (tel: 9380 9966; www.gingerandsmart.com; Mon–Sat 10am–6pm, Sun 11am–5pm) for their eclectic fabrics; and celebrity favourites **Camilla and Marc** (8/2–16 Glenmore Road; tel: 9331 1133; www.camillaandmarc.com; Mon–Wed and Fri, Sat 10am–6pm, Thur 10am–7pm, Sun 11am–5pm), whose designs are worn by paparazzi prey including Elle Macpherson, Jennifer Lopez and Lindsay Lohan.

Art galleries

Also on this stretch are some excellent galleries. At No. 20, **Gallery Savah** (tel: 9360 9979; www.savah.com.au; Tue–Sun 11am–6pm) represents a selection of notable Australian and Aboriginal artists, while at No. 19, **Maunsell Wickes at Barry Stern Gallery** (tel: 9331 4676; www.maunsellwickes.com; Tue–Sat 11am–5.30pm, Sun noon–5pm) sprawls through three 1840s terrace houses, with nine exhibition spaces featuring a range of painters, printmakers, sculptors and ceramicists.

If all this artwork is making you thirsty, take a break at **Jackies and Raw Bar II**, see ❶, on the corner.

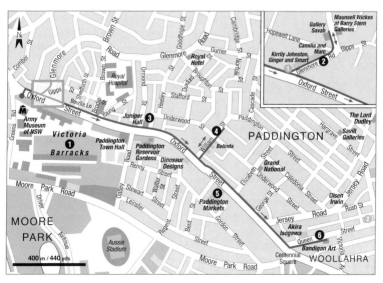

Chi-chi boutique

JUNIPER HALL

Head southeast on Oxford Street for about 300 metres, passing the 1891 Italianate **Paddington Town Hall** on the opposite side of the street, to reach the intersection with Ormond Street, location of Paddington's finest historic building, **Juniper Hall** ❸, constructed by Robert Cooper, ex-convict and gin distiller. His elegant villa – named after gin's key ingredient – was completed in 1824. Juniper Hall is Australia's oldest surviving villa, although the magnificent views it once enjoyed of Sydney Harbour, Botany Bay and the Blue Mountains have been eaten up by urban sprawl. The building belongs to the National Trust (www.nsw.nationaltrust.org.au) and currently houses a French antiques store.

Directly opposite, on the corner of Oxford and Oatley Streets, is the former

Paddington beer

Tucked away in the backstreets of Paddington is an impressive collection of British-style pubs, all with quality restaurants as well as cosy bars. If you're in the mood for a pint with a side order of nostalgia, choose between the Four in Hand (105 Sutherland Street; tel: 9362 1999; www.fourinhand.com.au), the Royal Hotel (237 Glenmore Road; tel: 9331 2604; www.royalhotel.com.au) and the Lord Dudley (236 Jersey Road; tel: 9327 5399; www.lorddudley.com.au).

Paddington Reservoir, now reinvented as a tranquil sunken garden fringed with a hanging garden canopy. It's a lovely example of urban reinvention, and a favourite spot for locals.

WILLIAM STREET

Around 300 metres further along and on the left is **William Street** ❹, a terraced strip that is home to many of Paddington's biggest names in fashion. Collette Dinnigan, probably Australia's most internationally acclaimed fashion designer, has stepped away from the business and shut up shop here, but look out for **Belinda** at No.39 (tel: 9380 8728; www.belinda.com.au; Mon–Wed and Fri 10am–6pm, Thur 10am–9pm, Sat 10am–5pm, Sun noon–5pm), whose boutiques are known for their well-edited choice of European labels.

PADDINGTON MARKETS

Back on Oxford Street and slightly further south are **Paddington Markets** ❺ (395 Oxford Street; tel: 9331 2923; www.paddingtonmarkets.com.au; Sat 10am–5pm), held in the grounds of the Uniting Church since 1973. Sydney's most famous market has been the launching point for many great Australian labels, including Australia's best-known jeweller, **Dinosaur Designs** (339 Oxford Street; tel: 9361 3776; www.dinosaurdesigns.com.au; Mon–Wed and Fri 9.30am–5.30pm, Thur 9.30am–8pm,

Paddington Markets

Sat 10am–5pm, Sun noon–4pm), who are known for their brilliantly coloured resin jewellery and still operate from around the corner.

There are around 250 stalls here, selling everything from pet accessories to homemade jams, but the emphasis is on fashions by young designers. The market also has a range of food stalls and a children's play area. The crowds will slow you right down, so be prepared for this.

WOOLLAHRA

Return to Oxford Street and browse the shops as you head southeast to **Queen Street ⑥**, another of the area's great shopping strips, about 500 metres away. The area you are now in is Woollahra, where the feel is different; the shady trees and larger terraces signal serious money, as does the shopping.

Queen Street is lined with boutiques and galleries, including **Akira Isogawa** (12a Queen Street; tel: 9361 5221; www.akira.au.com; Mon–Sat 10.30am–6pm, Sun 11am–4pm), one of Australia's most acclaimed designers. Artworks of a different type can be found at the **Dickerson Gallery** (34 Queen Street, Woollahra; tel: 9363 3358; www.dickersongallery.com.au; Tue–Sat 11am–5pm, Sun 1–5.30pm), which showcases established and up and coming Australian artists. Some of Paddington's best galleries are located away from the main drag. Art-lovers should check out **Savill Galleries** (156 Hargrave Street; tel:

02 9327 8311; www.savill.com.au) and **Olsen Irwin Gallery** (63 Jersey Road; tel: 9327 3922; www.olsenirwin.com) for 20th-century Australian art.

You might like to grab a bite to eat and a refreshing beverage at the Woollahra Hotel, home to **Bistro Moncur**, see ②.

Food and Drink

① JACKIES CAFE

122 Oxford Street, Paddington; tel: 9380 9818; Sun–Mon 7.30am–3pm; $–$$
Once a much-loved Bondi favourite, Jackie's has retained its popularity since relocating to a chic new home, where fashionistas rest their Jimmy Choo shoes either in the large courtyard or the cool sandstone-lined interior. Foodwise, choose from the Italian-influenced cafe menu, or the super-fresh sushi and sashimi.

② BISTRO MONCUR

Woollahra Hotel, 116 Queen Street; 02 9327 9713; www.woollahrahotel.com. au; Mon–Thur noon–3pm & 6pm–Late, Fri noon–3pm & 5.30pm–Late, Sat noon–3pm & 5.30pm–10.30pm, Sun noon–3pm & 5.30pm–9pm; $$–$$$
Although actually a pub, Bistro Moncur has a jazzy Parisian feel that is matched by the superb food on offer – far superior to your average pub grub. If you are not in the mood for a full sit-down affair, its more casual option, The Terrace, serves Wagyu burgers and spatchcock.

Picturesque Shark Beach (Nielsen Park Beach)

HERMITAGE FORESHORE

The easy Hermitage foreshore route, from Rose Bay to Nielsen Park, is one of the prettiest stretches of Sydney's bush-fringed harbour foreshore. Bring a swimsuit to take advantage of the little beaches along the way.

DISTANCE: 3km (1.75 miles)
TIME: A half-/full day
START: Foreshore Reserve
END: Vaucluse House
POINTS TO NOTE: Take bus No. 324 from town (see www.131500.com. au) and ask to be let off at Kincoppal. At the end of the walk, you can either take the 324 back to town from outside Vaucluse House, or go on to route 8 (see page 68) by hopping onto the 324 on the opposite side of the road for the short trip to Watsons Bay.

de-sac, you'll find the entrance to the **Foreshore Reserve ❶**. A signposted walk was established through the reserve in 1984.

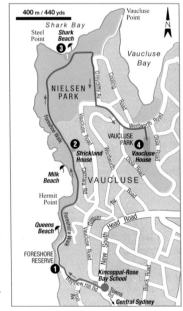

Alight from the No. 324 bus when you see an impressive edifice, reminiscent of a fortified French château, on the corner of New South Head Road and Bayview Hill Road. Originally built as a convent, it now houses one of Sydney's most exclusive private girls' schools, Kincoppal.

Head down Bayview Hill Road – staying to the right when Tivoli Avenue splits away left. Where it culminates in a cul-

Making use of the water   *Strickland House*

FORESHORE WALK

This 2km (1.25-mile) dirt track takes you through leafy bush and right along the harbour foreshore. In addition to offering stunning views stretching back to the Harbour Bridge and the Opera House, the walk is the only way to access some of Sydney's least-known beaches: tiny strips of white sand including Queens Beach, Hermit Point Beach and Milk Beach. These make great rest stops along the way and, on weekdays especially, you will probably have them all to yourself.

Towards the end of the walk, the trail borders the green lawns of **Strickland House** ❷ (not open to the public), which had a cameo role in Baz Luhrmann's film *Australia*. The Italianate mansion was designed in 1856 by John Hilly for John Hosking, the first Lord Mayor of Sydney.

The foreshore walk culminates at the picturesque **Shark Beach** ❸ (popularly known as Nielsen Park Beach). Don't let the name – or the shark net – worry you too much, shark attacks in Sydney Harbour are extremely rare. **Nielsen Park Café & Restaurant**, see ❶, is a good pitstop.

Shell middens and hand stencils testify to the presence of the Cadigal people in the days before settlement. The beach was once privately owned, but an incident in the early 1900s, when boating picnickers were ordered off the beach and drowned while trying to find alternative shelter, added to the demand to make foreshore lands available to all.

VAUCLUSE HOUSE

From the top of Nielsen Park, it's a few minutes' walk south along Greycliffe Avenue and then east along Wentworth Road to reach the historic **Vaucluse House** ❹ (Wentworth Road; www.sydneylivingmuseums.com.au/vaucluse-house; Fri–Sun 9.30am–4pm; charge). A small stone cottage stood on this site as far back as 1803, but in 1827 the property was bought by William Charles Wentworth. He refurbished and extended it, and today the house, with its sweep of landscaped grounds and gardens, is one of the city's most significant historic sites.

Wentworth was an influential figure in the colony's earliest days, taking part in the first crossing of the Blue Mountains (see page 86) and forming the first university and independent newspaper.

(see page 86)

Food and drink

❶ NIELSEN PARK CAFÉ & RESTAURANT

Nielsen Park; tel: 9337 7333; www.nielsenpark.com.au; Tue–Fri 8.30am–4pm, Sat–Sun 8am–4pm, kiosk daily 8am–4pm & Fri–Sun 4pm–sunset; $–$$

This is a year-round favourite for breakfast and lunch. Start with a baked pie of slow-cooked free-range lamb shank, borlotti beans, green peas and gremolata, but leave room for one of the delicious desserts. Or just get fish and chips.

Banksias, typical of the vegetation in this area

SOUTH HEAD AND WATSONS BAY

Guarding the entrance to Sydney Harbour, South Head has two very different sides: one wild and windswept, the other with sheltered coves. Military buffs will love the area's rich history; others will enjoy some of the best views in Sydney.

> **DISTANCE:** 4.5km (2.75 miles)
> **TIME:** A half-/full day
> **START:** Macquarie Lighthouse
> **END:** Hornby Lighthouse
> **POINTS TO NOTE:** This route can be combined with the previous one (see page 66); simply catch bus No. 324 for the short trip from Shark Beach to Christison Park. Alternatively, catch the No. 324 bus from town. After the tour, catch a ferry from Watsons Bay Wharf back to Circular Quay.

An easy clifftop walk starting at Christison Park leads you along first the ocean side of South Head, then the calmer harbour side. The area, formerly owned by the army and now a national park, remains rich in military relics.

MACQUARIE LIGHTHOUSE

The most impressive building on the first section of the walk is the **Macquarie Lighthouse ❶**, Australia's old-est lighthouse. A beacon stood on this site as early as 1791. Fired by wood, it was used to guide vessels to the harbour entrance at night. In 1816, work began on a lighthouse, designed by convict architect Francis Greenway. Governor Macquarie was so pleased with his work that, on its completion in 1818, he granted Greenway a pardon and the ex-con went on to design some of the colony's most important buildings.

Unfortunately, the sandstone used to build the lighthouse quickly began to erode, and the tower had to be held together with iron bands. In 1883, work commenced on a replacement, designed by James Barnet, and this is the building that can be seen today, although remnants of the first lighthouse are also visible nearby.

SIGNAL STATION

Northeast of the lighthouse is the **Signal Station ❷**. In its infancy, Sydney depended heavily on supply ships from England. For the first two years

Watsons Bay from above

Yacht coming into the bay

of the colony, a party of marines was sent to Botany Bay each week to see whether any ships had arrived, unaware that the settlement had moved to Port Jackson (the harbour containing Sydney Harbour, North Harbour and Middle Harbour and named by Captain James Cook, when he discovered the inlet in 1770). In 1790, a more efficient approach was adopted, and a lookout post was erected on South Head.

The existing Signal Station dates back to 1842. In 1854, with the outbreak of the Crimean War, a cannon was placed below the Signal Station, to alert the colony in case a Russian fleet arrived at the heads. The adjacent gun fortifications and tunnels were added in 1892, and upgraded during World War II.

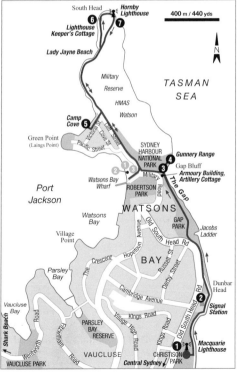

About 100 metres further on is a plaque that commemorates the wreck of the *Dunbar*. In 1857, the *Dunbar*, a ship from England, was wrecked on the rocks just south of the towering headland. Of the 122 people on board, only one survived: crewman James Johnson, who was miraculously lifted by the surging water on to a rock ledge.

From here, the walk continues along the cliff's edge, past a verdant gully filled with cabbage palms, tree ferns and figs, to **The Gap** ❸, the scenic ocean cliff that is also, sadly, one of Sydney's major suicide spots.

Gun emplacement at Camp Cove

GUNNERY RANGE

About 10 metres past The Gap, steps to the right take you to the **Gunnery Range ❹**. In 1894, four obsolete muzzle-loading 80-pounder guns were mounted here as a practice battery. A year later, the School of Gunnery was relocated from Middle Head to South Head. The gunnery was dismantled in 1917, but the parapets and the circular rails that the guns traversed are still visible.

Near the lookout is a plaque marked 'Guns and Roses', which indicates the path to Inner South Head. On the way, you will pass the remains of some of the 30 buildings that once stood here. Although the scrubby native vegetation is taking over, keen observers may spot a few clues to the area's old life, including walls, tiles, bricks and former fountains. The only original building still standing is the **Armoury Building**, dating back to 1838, which marks the end of the path.

SANDY BEACHES

At the end of the path, turn right and follow the signs for the South Head Heritage Trail. This will bring you to **Camp Cove ❺**, a sheltered beach that is a great place for a swim. The beach has a kiosk selling cool drinks and ice creams. The Heritage Trail (at this point a cobblestone roadway), which was once used to transport guns and hardware from Camp Cove Wharf to the South Head batteries, begins at the far end of the beach. The trail takes you past yet another popular swimming spot – **Lady Jayne Beach** – one of Sydney's three designated nudist beaches.

As you walk you'll see that most of the vegetation on South Head is heathland and native scrub. Typical plants include banksias, smouldering specimens of which were used by Aboriginal

Invasion fears

Although it is hard to imagine why anyone would want to attack a remote penal settlement, the threat of invasion was ever-present in colonists' minds, which led to the fortification of South Head. Just where the attacks were supposed to come from changed with the years. In the 1820s, fear of the French (England's traditional enemy) began to be replaced by fear of the US, which was growing in power. Fear reached fever pitch in 1839, when six North American ships entered the harbour by night, and were not spotted until the sun rose the next day. That led to the decision to fortify Pinchgut (now Fort Denison), Bradley's Head and South Head. In 1853, suspicion once again fell on the French, thanks to their decision to colonise the South Pacific island of New Caledonia. The next year, however, enemy became ally, when Britain and France joined forces against Russia in the Crimean War.

The Lightkeeper's Cottage, with the red-and-white Hornby Lighthouse behind

tribes to transport fire from one place to another thousands of years ago.

LIGHTHOUSE KEEPER'S COTTAGE

The wreck of the *Dunbar* led to the decision to build a lighthouse on South Head. Fittingly, the first lighthouse keeper to live here was none other than Henry Johnson, the brother of the *Dunbar*'s sole survivor. The lighthouse and the adjacent **Lighthouse Keeper's Cottage** ❻ were designed by Alexander Dawson.

HORNBY LIGHTHOUSE

Further along the path you will come to the **Hornby Lighthouse** ❼ itself, with its distinctive red-and-white vertical stripes (lighthouses are painted with unique patterns for the same reason that they have different flash sequences – so they can be individually identified by ships' captains). The name was chosen by the Governor, Sir William Denison, but its origin is uncertain; one theory suggests that it was named after British Admiral Horatio Hornby, who also happened to be Lady Denison's father. Originally lit by 16 kerosene lamps, it was converted to gas in 1904, and then electrified in 1948.

After the lighthouse, the track loops around, returning you to the path. Head back to Camp Cove, then go southeast on Cliff Street to reach Robertson Park. Here you can recover with fish and chips at **Doyles**, see ❶ and ❷, or the **Watsons Bay Hotel**, see ❸, before heading to Watsons Bay Wharf at the foot of the park, and catching a ferry back to the Circular Quay.

Food and drink

❶ DOYLES ON THE BEACH

11 Marine Parade, Watsons Bay; tel: 9337 2007; www.doyles.com.au; Mon–Fri noon–3pm, Sat–Sun 12pm–4pm & daily 5.30pm–9pm (later in summer); $$$

❷ DOYLES ON THE WHARF

The Wharf, Watsons Bay; tel: 9337 6214; www.doyles.com.au; daily 11am–5pm (later at weekends and during summer); $$–$$$

The Doyle family have been selling seafood at Watsons Bay since 1885, and today's visitors can choose from two outlets. The more formal Doyles on the Beach has superb, if expensive, seafood platters; Doyles on the Wharf is a more casual eat-in or takeaway joint.

❸ WATSONS BAY HOTEL

1 Military Road, Watsons Bay; tel: 9337 5444; www.watsonsbayhotel.com.au; daily 7am–late; $–$$

Summer weekends at the 'Watto' are a Sydney institution. Steaks, salads and fish and chips in the shady beer garden, washed down by cold beer, are the perfect way to while away an afternoon. If it's hot, head to Camp Cove beach for a quick dip between courses (pre-beer/wine, of course).

BONDI AND BEYOND

Sydney's most famous beach is just the beginning; stretching south from Bondi is a chain of beaches, linked by a coastal walk that offers spectacular ocean panoramas. This route takes in rugged cliffs and pockets of subtropical forest, with plenty of opportunities to dive into the ocean along the way.

DISTANCE: 5.5km (3.5 miles)
TIME: A half-/full day
START: Bondi Beach
END: Coogee Beach
POINTS TO NOTE: This route can get very crowded, particularly on fine weekends, so tackling it on a weekday is recommended. If you prefer a shorter walk, the first section, to Bronte Beach, is just 1.5km (1 mile). Stop there for a coffee before returning the way you came. Whether you are doing the whole walk or just part of it, pack your swimming costume, drinking water, high-factor sunscreen and a hat. To get to Bondi from town, take bus 380, 382 or 333 (the last is the fastest, as it is prepay only). If you are finishing the walk at Coogee, buses 372, 373 and 374 will take you back to town.

The residents of Sydney's posh eastern suburbs have a reputation for being pleased with themselves, and on a balmy spring day it's not hard to see why. As you meander along the spectacular clifftop walk – linking no fewer than five of Sydney's favourite beaches, not to mention a couple of popular ocean baths – it's hard to think of a better way to start the day.

This route offers a range of bathing opportunities – but if you opt for a swim off any of the beaches, be sure to always swim between the flags and if the shark alarm goes, hotfoot it out of the water immediately.

BONDI BEACH

Australia's most famous beach, **Bondi ❶**, is a source of both pride and exasperation to locals. They love the Art Deco buildings along Campbell Parade, the main road that runs alongside the beach, but hate the traffic that clogs it. They love the concerts and events held on grassy Bondi Park and in the Bondi Surf Pavilion, but resent the crowds that come along. Most of all, however, they love the gently curving beach and the brilliant blue water that washes up against it.

Lifeguards in their distinctive bathers

Start at Notts Avenue at the south end of Bondi Beach, and walk to the end of the road, past the **Bondi Icebergs Club ❷** (1 Notts Avenue; www.icebergs.com.au; Mon–Fri 11am–late, Sat–Sun 9am–late; charge), a local icon. The baths themselves date back to the 1880s, and have been home to the Icebergs since 1929. The club's season begins in early winter, when a tonne of ice is deposited in the pool. Since a controversial redevelopment in 2001, the club is also home to one of Sydney's most glamorous venues, **Icebergs Dining Room and Bar**, see ❶.

Past Icebergs, stairs lead down through the rocky cove known as **The Boot**. Climb back up the cliff to earn an amazing vista from **Mackenzie's Point**. Public toilets are available here in Marks Park. If you look carefully, you can see Aboriginal rock carvings of a shark or whale next to the path south of the point. (Whales migrate along this coast June–early July and Sept–Nov.)

Each November, the Bondi-to-Bronte walk hosts the excellent Sculpture by the Sea exhibition, when contemporary works are exhibited on land and sometimes sea.

TAMARAMA BEACH

Continuing around the path brings you to **Tamarama Beach ❸**, known as Glamarama in tribute to the chic eastern-suburbs types who congre-

Artworks set out for Sculpture by the Sea

gate here. Directly behind the beach is the pocket-sized **Tamarama Park**, a verdant spot that was once home to Wonderland City, Sydney's first amusement park. These days it has a cafe, toilets and play equipment, and lush subtropical vegetation. If you are planning on taking a dip, stay strictly within the flags; Tamarama is known for its dangerous rips.

BRONTE BEACH

Following the path around the next headland, you come to **Bronte Beach** ❹, named not for the family of writers but for the English Admiral Horatio Nelson, who was also the Duke of Bronte. This beach is a favourite with eastern-suburbs families, thanks to its seawater baths, sprawling parklands with barbecue facilities, toilets and a little steam train for the kids. The small strip of cafes opposite the beach is a great place to relax with a coffee… if you can find a seat, that is. Try **Jenny's Cafe**, see ❷.

WAVERLEY CEMETERY

Cut through the car park behind the seawater baths and continue along the cliff edge to what may be the most spectacularly located cemetery in the world. The 16 hectares (40 acres) of **Waverley Cemetery** ❺ (St Thomas Street, Bronte; www.waverley.nsw. gov.au/cemetery; daily 7am–dusk;

free) boast over 50,000 burial spots, ranging from simple grassy plots to elaborate tombs. Among the famous Australians resting here are poets Henry Lawson and Dorothea McKellar, aviator Lawrence Hargrave, test cricketer Victor Trumper and champion swimmer Fanny Durack.

CLOVELLY BEACH

Leave the cemetery and follow the path past Clovelly Bowling Club to reach **Clovelly Beach** ❻. At the bottom of a long, narrow bay, lying between two rocky ridges and protected by a breakwater, the beach's calm waters make it a favourite with families. Snorkellers also head here to check out the local marine life, and concrete platforms on both sides of the bay are popular places for sunbathers, with a small pool set into the western side beneath the surf lifesaving club, where there is also a good cafe, **Seasalt**, see ❸.

COOGEE BEACH

From the surf lifesaving club, cut through the car park to rejoin the walk at Gordon's Bay, where the rocks are another popular spot for sunbathers and swimmers. A steep run of stairs makes this the most strenuous section of the walk, but once around the bay, you emerge onto the bare headland of Coogee. From here you can either walk down to **Coogee**

Bronte Beach   *Sculpture by the Sea exhibit*

Beach ❼, or continue on to two popular baths on the rock platforms located just south of the beach.

Coogee's saltwater baths

The first pool you come to, **McIver's Baths** (Grant Reserve, Beach Street; daily sunrise to sunset; charge), is better known as the Women's Baths. The secluded 20-metre ocean pool, set on a rock platform, has been used solely by women and children since the late 1800s. For a nominal entry fee, women can relax in a secluded, well-screened space. Its counterpart, the men-only Giles Baths, was closed in the 1970s after suffering severe storm damage.

Further along the walk are **Wylie's Baths** (Grant Reserve, Beach Street; daily: Oct–early Apr 7am–7pm, early Apr–Sept 7am–5pm; charge), built in 1907 by champion swimmer Henry Alexander Wylie. The baths were one of the first mixed-gender bathing pools in Australia, and were used by Wylie's daughter Wilhelmina who, along with Fanny Durack, was one of Australia's first two female Olympic swimmers. The baths have a 45-metre pool with a sweeping 180-degree view, and also offer yoga classes.

Food and drink

❶ ICEBERGS DINING ROOM AND BAR

1 Notts Avenue, Bondi Beach; tel: 9365 9000; www.idrb.com; Restaurant Tue–Sat noon–evening & Sun 10am–evening, Terrace Tues–Sun 7.30am–2pm; $$$

If all Icebergs had to offer was the view, it would still be worth a visit. Throw in chic interiors, attentive service, a fantastic wine list and simple yet perfectly finished Mediterranean food, and you have a quintessential Sydney dining experiences. For a cheaper treat, have a cocktail or two instead – just remember to 'frock up'.

❷ JENNY'S CAFE

485 Bronte Road, Bronte; tel: 9389 7498; daily 7am–5pm; $

Few Sydney cafes are as busy as the small venues squashed next to each other opposite Bronte Beach. Jenny's Cafe has a relaxed, homely feel, as well as an array of freshly pressed juices, cakes and coffee.

❸ SEASALT

1 Donnellan Circuit, Clovelly; tel: 9664 5344; www.seasaltcafe.com.au; Mon–Fri 9am–3.30pm, Sat–Sun 8.30am–4pm; $–$$

It may be less glamorous than Bondi or Bronte, but Clovelly has at least one chic cafe that can compete with its neighbours. Tucked below the lifesaving club, Seasalt has an interior designed by the acclaimed team of Burley Katon Halliday, and serves salads, sandwiches, pasta and seafood.

Captain Cook taking possession of New South Wales in 1770 in the name of the British crown

BOTANY BAY

This tour travels to the birthplace of European Australia – the bay where Captain Cook anchored over 200 years ago, so starting a new chapter in the continent's history. Bushwalks, picnics and monuments are all part of this historic day trip.

DISTANCE: 65km (40 miles)
TIME: A full day
START/END: Sydney
POINTS TO NOTE: You will need a car to do this complete route, which takes in two headlands located at either side of Botany Bay. If you are short of time, or you don't want to drive, you can take a direct bus (No. 394 from Circular Quay) to La Perouse. Sunday is the best time to visit La Perouse – that's when the fort is open, and on Sunday afternoons from 1.30pm you can enjoy a distinctive and charming tradition that started in the 1920s – a burly snake-charmer showing off his reptilian mates near the bus stop. The distance above reflects the full route (including to Kurnell), marked in red on the map.

Botany Bay is where the European chapter of Australian history began. At 3pm on 29 April 1770, Captain James Cook stepped ashore from the *Endeavour* to claim the 'Great South Land' for Britain. The anchorage was named Botany Bay after more than 3,000 new botanical specimens were collected by the expedition's naturalist, Joseph Banks, during the eight days the ship was moored here. In 1788, the First Fleet also stopped off briefly, but finding the site unsuitable for a permanent settlement, moved on to Sydney Cove. The name Botany Bay became 19th-century shorthand for the terrors that awaited convicts transported down under.

TOWARDS BOTANY BAY

Allow about an hour for the drive to Kurnell. Head south from Sydney on the Eastern Distributor. Turn left onto General Holmes Drive and follow the signs to Rockdale. Turn right onto President Avenue to join Princes Highway. At Kogarah, take Rocky Point Road, following the sign for Ramsgate and Cronulla, and cross the Georges River to Taren Point. Turn left at Captain Cook Drive, following the sign for **Kurnell**. From here, it's another 10km (6 miles)

Boardwalk on Botany Bay

until you arrive at **Kamay Botany Bay National Park** (Kamay being the indigenous name for the bay). You can drive into the park (a fee applies), or park on the street outside.

The drive is not a particularly scenic one, winding through red-roofed suburbs to the Kurnell Peninsula. Many of Sydney's most unloved projects – from huge oil refineries to a desalination plant – are on display here. However, Botany Bay National Park – 436 hectares (1,000 acres) of coastal cliffs, heath, woodland and quiet beaches – remains a popular destination for weekend picnics, and plenty of swimmers are happy to plunge into the water within sight of the refineries.

CAPTAIN COOK'S LANDING SITE

Head down to the water to join the **Monument Track ❶**, a 1km (0.6-mile) wheelchair-accessible walk along the coast to the park's visitor centre. On the way you pass monuments including the Solander Monument (1914), the Captain Cook Obelisk (built in 1870 to mark the *Endeavour*'s 1770 landing place), the Sir Joseph Banks Memorial (1947), and a memorial to Seaman Forby Sutherland, the first European known to be buried on the continent. The **Visitor Centre ❷** (Botany Bay National Park, Cape Solander Drive; tel: 9668 2000; daily 9.30am–4.30pm) is the place to pick up park maps, and also has toilet facilities and a canteen selling ice creams and snacks.

Bush walks

Several walks start on the far side of the centre's car park, including the 1km (0.6-mile) **Yena Track**. The track is marked with signs about local flora, including how the local Gwyeagal people used plants such as the wattle: its fibre for utensils, its leaves as fish poison, its unripe seeds as soap and its ripe roasted seeds as fuel. Particularly on a hot day, when the cicadas are shrilling and kooka-

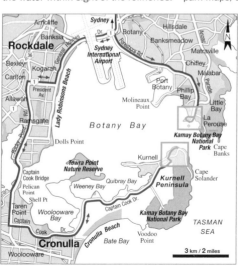

burras calling, walking past the scribbly gums and through the heath, it is easy to imagine how strange this landscape must have seemed to the newly arrived Europeans.

The Yena Track leads to a scenic coastal outlook, from where you can either return to the Visitor Centre via the **Muru Track**, or continue along the clifftop to join the **Cape Baily Coast Walk**, an 8km (5-mile) stroll past dunes, heathlands and swamps. The views are magnificent, and in June and early July and from September to November, you may even spot migrating whales.

LA PEROUSE

From Kurnell, you can either return to the city the way you came, or head right around the bay to **La Perouse** on the opposite heads. Drive back towards the airport, and follow the signs to the right for Port Botany. These will take you onto Foreshore Road, past ranks of container storage. Turn right at Bun-nerong Road (which joins Anzac Parade just before the peninsula) and follow the road until you reach La Perouse, where beaches, bushland, historic buildings and fish-and-chips shops are jumbled together at the end of the peninsula. The loop road on the headland was originally a circular track, forming part of the tram terminus, before the trams were decommissioned in 1961.

The suburb is named after the Comte de La Pérouse, the French naval commander who arrived in Botany Bay just eight days after Captain Phillip and the First Fleet in 1788. The meeting was cordial enough, though the British were unable to assist the French with food, as they were running short themselves. La Pérouse set up a camp on the north shore, and when he left, entrusted his journals and letters to the British ship *Sirius*, which was returning to Europe. This was a fortunate move, as the French ships disappeared after departing Botany Bay for New Caledonia and the wrecks were only discovered in 1964.

Historic buildings

The round tower at the start of the loop is the **Macquarie Watchtower 3**, constructed in the 1820s to house a small squad of soldiers stationed on the point to prevent smuggling. At the bottom of the loop lies **Bare Island 4** (tel: 9311 3379; charge), which got its name from Captain Cook's description of it as 'a small bare island'.

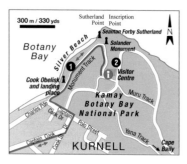

Bare Island panorama

The island, now linked to the mainland by a footbridge, had fortifications designed by colonial architect James Barnet added in 1885. For 50 years it was used as a retirement home for war veterans, until it was handed over to the New South Wales Parks and Wildlife Service in 1963. Tours take place on Sundays at 1.30pm, 2.30pm and 3.30pm. Tickets can be bought from the La Perouse Museum a little further around the loop.

La Perouse Museum

The building housing the **La Perouse Museum** ❺ (Wed–Sun 10am–4pm; charge) was constructed in 1882, as a cable station, and housed workers operating the 1876 undersea telegraph line to New Zealand. It now contains maps, scientific instruments and relics linked to the French explorers.

Near the museum is the **La Perouse Monument**, an obelisk erected in 1825 by the French, and a memorial marking the grave of one of the expedition's scientists, Father Receveur.

HENRY HEAD TRACK

From here, treat yourself to some fish and chips from **Danny's Seafood**, see ❶ or, if you are still feeling energetic, take the signposted 5km (3-mile) walk along the **Henry Head Track** from La Perouse Museum to the Endeavour Lighthouse. The track passes through coastal heath, angophora forest and military fortifications. From the lighthouse, there are fine views across the bay. Along the walk, information signs explain the history of the area, including the squatters' camp that housed at least 330 people during the 1930s depression. Camps such as this one were found on coastal land around Sydney, with huts built out of whatever material was available, such as corrugated iron, hessian and earth.

To return to Sydney city centre, head north on Anzac Parade via Kingsford.

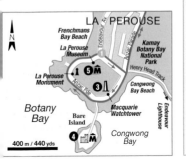

Food and drink

❶ DANNY'S SEAFOOD

1605 Anzac Parade, La Perouse; tel: 9311 4116; www.dannys.net.au; daily 11am–late; $–$$

Danny's has been serving up seafood by the beach for approximately 30 years. Downstairs, the chefs dole out straightforward fish and chips – eat at one of the outside tables, or take it with you to the beach – while upstairs you will be offered a more sophisticated seafood experience.

Manly's fabulous beach

THE SPIT TO MANLY

In a city blessed with an abundance of fabulous foreshore walks, the Spit to Manly route is the most magnificent of all. The trail through swathes of untouched bushland offers magnificent harbour panoramas and secluded beaches, and culminates in one of Sydney's favourite seaside playgrounds.

DISTANCE: 9.25km (5.75 miles)
TIME: A full day
START: Ellery's Punt Reserve
END: Shelly Beach
POINTS TO NOTE: This foreshore route is strenuous, involving rough tracks and lots of stairs. There are no refreshments en route, so be sure to pack some water and snacks along with your swimsuit, hat and sunscreen. To get to the starting point, you can either catch a bus from Wynyard station (Nos 140 or 190; for more information, visit www.131500. com.au or call 131 500), or take a taxi. From Manly, catch a ferry back to the city.

This route around the northern side of the Middle Harbour offers an insight into two very different aspects of how Sydneysiders make use of their harbour. The foreshore walk takes you through a landscape that in parts is little changed from when Europeans first arrived. However, Manly, the seaside suburb famously 'seven miles from Sydney, a thousand miles from care', has long been a place for locals to escape the big smoke. Allow about three hours for the foreshore walk, and a few extra hours for exploring what Manly has to offer.

ELLERY'S PUNT RESERVE

Ask your bus or taxi driver to drop you at the southern end of Spit Bridge, and take the walkway on the western side of the bridge. At the far end there is a staircase leading down to a grassy clearing and popular fishing spot called **Ellery's Punt Reserve ❶**. In the 1850s, before the construction of the first bridge in 1924, Manly was connected to The Spit by a punt that carried pedestrians, horses, carts and tram passengers. The tram service ceased in 1939, but the walkway follows the old tram route for 200 metres towards Fishers Bay.

CLONTARF BEACH

A 20-minute walk will bring you to **Clontarf Beach ❷**, a family-friendly spot with picnic shelters, toilets and other facilities. Clontarf's moment of fame came in

1868, when it was the site of an assassination attempt on Queen Victoria's second son, Prince Alfred; the bullet was deflected from the prince's spine by his rubber braces. Stairs at the far end of Clontarf Beach, which take you up to the path, may be inaccessible at high tide. An alternative route, via Monash Crescent, is clearly marked.

GROTTO POINT

The next hour of the walk is the most strenuous, with the route winding up and down hills and frequent stairs. If you need to cool off, there are steps down to tiny **Castle Rock Beach ❸**. Alternatively, continue along the path to **Grotto Point**, where a First Fleet survey party camped in January 1788. A signpost shows you the way to the **Grotto Point Lighthouse**, a 1km (0.6-mile) detour. The building,

which resembles a Greek chapel, was built in 1911 and is still used to guide ships in the harbour. Return to the path and, after a short while, you will come to a clearing on your right that contains a number of **Aboriginal engravings**.

FORTY BASKETS BEACH

After continuing uphill again, the path takes a detour through a number of suburban streets, including Ogilvy Road, Vista Avenue and Bareena Drive, before coming to **Tania Park**, named after one of the area's first local celebrities, Tania Verstak, who was crowned Miss Australia in 1961.

On the far side of the park, follow signs and descend to **Forty Baskets Beach ❹**, a name commemorating a catch of 40 baskets of fish that were sent to Sudanese troops encamped at the North Head Quarantine Station in 1885. You

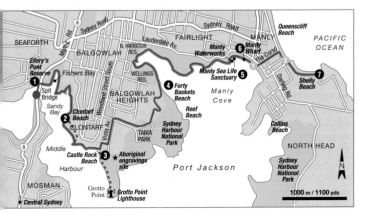

Shelly Beach

have now re-entered suburbia, travelling through Wellings Reserve and North Harbour Reserve. Continue along the opposite side of the cove to Fairlight Beach; the path from here around to Manly is very popular, due to its gentle slope.

OCEANWORLD

Once you round the corner into Manly Cove, you come to **Manly Sea Life Sanctuary 5** (West Esplanade; www.manlysealifesanctuary.com.au; daily 9.30am–5pm; charge), a 4 million-litre (880,000-gallon) aquarium. Along with the touch pools and main tank, there are sessions featuring Australia's most dangerous animals, including snakes, spiders and crocodiles. The biggest attraction, however, is the opportunity to dive with sharks, for which bookings are essential (tel: 8251 7878). Right next door is **Manly Waterworks** (Cnr West Esplanade and Commonwealth Parade; www.manlywaterworks.com.au; charge; seasonal opening) a playpark with giant slides that is very popular with children.

MANLY

About 200 metres the Sea Life Sanctuary is **Manly Wharf 6**. This is where the ferry from Circular Quay pulls in and also forms an entertainment hub, with pubs and restaurants. Grab a bite at one of the restaurants lining The Esplanade, such as **Out of Africa**, see ❶, or head down The Corso, a lively pedestrian zone that continues all the way to the surf side of Manly. At Manly, Norfolk pines line the long stretch of beach. Plenty of eateries line the street opposite the beach here, such as **Whitewater**, see ❷.

Head right for another short scenic walk along Manly Cove to peaceful **Shelly Beach 7**. When you're ready, stroll back along The Corso to Manly Wharf, and hop on a ferry back to Circular Quay.

Food and drink

❶ OUT OF AFRICA

43–5 East Esplanade, Manly; tel: 9977 0055; www.outofafrica.com.au; Mon–Thu 6pm–10.30pm, Fri noon–10.30pm, Sat–Sun 9am–10.30pm; $–$$

The orange walls and zebra-striped banquette are eye-catching, but the food is equally attention-grabbing. Moroccan tagines are the speciality of the house, but the menu includes many dishes from across the continent, including South African *sosaties* (kebabs).

❷ WHITEWATER

35 South Steyne, Manly; tel: 9977 0322; www.whitewaterrestaurant.com.au; Mon–Fri 11am–late, Sat–Sun 8am–late; $–$$

It's been a long time since Manly's culinary offerings were limited to fish and chips. These days, the area has many sophisticated diners like this one. Seafood is a specialty, from fresh oysters to hiramasa kingfish and whitebait fritters.

Palm Beach

NORTHERN BEACHES

*Known to locals as The Peninsula, postcodes from the Northern Beaches are
among Sydney's most exclusive addresses. Characterised by sweeping beaches,
palm trees, chic cafes and expensive homes, this is one of the city's most popular
summer haunts.*

DISTANCE: 20km (12.5 miles)
TIME: A full day
START: Bungan Beach
END: Palm Beach
POINTS TO NOTE: The L90 bus runs
from the city to Palm Beach but,
depending on traffic, the trip can take
up to two hours. The best way to explore
the Northern Beaches is definitely by
car, although you will need to have lots
of coins for the parking meters.

Northern Beaches' residents like to think
of themselves as being a breed apart,
and when you drive up there, it is not
hard to see why – The Peninsula does
feel like a different world. To millions of
British visitors, though, Palm Beach is
better known as Summer Bay – where
the outdoor scenes of popular soap
Home and Away are filmed.

Take the Northbridge exit from the
Harbour Bridge (after the North Sydney
exit) and follow the signs to Northbridge,
then continue on to the Eastern Valley
Way, all the way through **Forestville**. Just

20 metres after the Forest High School,
turn left onto the Wakehurst Parkway,
one of Sydney's most attractive roads.
For about 10km (6 miles) it cuts straight
through dense bushland, emerging at
the other end at the peaceful **Narrabeen
Lakes**. The road ends in a T-junction;
turn left onto Pittwater Road and head
towards Mona Vale shops, about 6km (4
miles) away.

BUNGAN BEACH

When you reach the shopping centre, veer left onto Barrenjoey Road as it
climbs the headland overlooking **Newport Beach**. At the crest of the hill, turn
right at Karlo Parade, then right into Bungan Road and park, if you can, on the
corner of Myola Road. A long, steep hill
descends to **Bungan Beach** ❶, one of
Sydney's most secluded sandy spots.

Returning the way you came, turn right
onto Barrenjoey Road and then immediately left into Beaconsfield Street, following the road all the way down to The
Peninsula's favourite pub. **The Newport
Arms Hotel**, see ❶ opened in 1880 and

The beach at Avalon

today has the Northern Beaches' largest outdoor screen, on which sporting events are shown.

BILGOLA BEACH AND AVALON

From the Newport Arms, head east along Queens Parade and rejoin Barrenjoey Road, turning left and continuing north until you see The Serpentine on your right, which leads to another of The Peninsula's hidden beaches. **Bilgola Beach** ❷ is nestled deep between high headlands in a small, subtropical rainforest of ferns and exotic blooms. The parking lot for Bilgola is the first right turn at the bottom of the hill. The beach has a kiosk selling basic refreshments.

As you leave the beach, turn right into The Serpentine, and wend your way around the bends back to Barrenjoey Road. Turning right at the next traffic lights will bring you to Avalon, the liveliest place on The Peninsula. Park where you can, then stroll down **Old Barrenjoey Road** ❸, home to a range of chic cafes and boutiques, including a fine bookstore-cum-café, **Bookoccino**, see ❷.

PALM BEACH

Keep heading north on Barrenjoey Road past Whale Beach – location of the renowned and wonderfully romantic **Jonah's**, see ❸ – to **Palm Beach** ❹, the area's most prestigious address. There are actually two beaches here, separated by the thin width of Barren-

joey Headland, but the surf beach on the right is Palm Beach proper. From the fa

The Basin

end of the more tranquil bayside beach on the left, you can access one of two tracks that lead to the **Barrenjoey Lighthouse**, perched 113 metres (371ft) above Broken Bay. Both are steep, but the lefthand path is much easier than the righthand path. Allow about an hour for the return journey, or break the walk at **The Greedy Goat**, see ❹.

THE BASIN

For something to eat at this point, stop at **Beach Road**, see, and then, from the wharf on the Pittwater side of Palm Beach, you can hop on a ferry operated by the Palm Beach Ferry Service (www.palmbeachferry.com.au) for a trip across Pittwater and Broken Bay. The ferry ride takes 20 minutes each way, and ferries arrive/leave every hour, so make sure you put enough money in the parking meter at Palm Beach.

Alight at West Head and take the walking track to **The Basin**, in the Ku-ring-gai Chase National Park. The Basin's collection of Aboriginal art is probably the most extensive on show in the Sydney area, and was created by the Gurringgai people who occupied this territory for over 20,000 years. To return to Sydney, take the ferry back to Palm Beach, then head back to the city centre via Pittwater Road and the Wakehurst Parkway.

Food and drink

❶ THE NEWPORT ARMS HOTEL
Corner of Beaconsfield and Kalinya streets, Newport; tel: 9997 4900; www.newportarms.com.au; Mon–Sat 10am–midnight, Sun 10am–10pm; $$–$$$
This pub has the largest beer garden in Australia, a green family-friendly space that is a great place to grab a burger.

❷ BOOKOCCINO
37A Old Barrenjoey Road; tel: 9973 1244; www.bookoccino.com; Mon–Sat 9.30am–6pm, Sun 10am–5pm; $
Brilliant books. Brilliant brews. Brilliant breakfasts. A bookshop and cafe that brings out the best of both. A quiet haven

amid all the frenetic sun-splattered action.

❸ JONAH'S
69 Bynya Road, Palm Beach; tel: 9974 5599; www.jonahs.com.au; daily 7.30am—9am, noon–2.30pm and 6.30pm–late; $$$
A meal at Jonah's offers one of the best views in Sydney, and the menu, slanted towards seafood, is also impressive.

❹ THE GREEDY GOAT
1093 Barrenjoey Road; tel: 9974 2555; www.thegreedygoat.com.au; daily 8am–3pm; $–$$
Funky food in a sensational atmosphere – think top breakfasts, cracking coffee, deli-style salads and healthy mains, washed down with BYO wine and homemade cakes.

Australian cockatoo in the Blue Mountains

BLUE MOUNTAINS

An expansive World Heritage–listed wilderness filled with deep gorges, plunging waterfalls and untouched bush, the Blue Mountains is one of NSW's most spectacular landscapes. It can be explored as a long day trip from Sydney, but two days will let you take in more of the area's highlights.

DISTANCE: 175km (109 miles)
TIME: Two days
START/END: Sydney
POINTS TO NOTE: It is possible to catch a train to Katoomba and the main villages, but to explore the area fully, you will need a car. The mountains are considerably cooler than Sydney, so take sufficient layers with you. No visit to the mountains is complete without a bush walk. A couple of short, easy options are included in the route; if you want something more challenging, you can obtain more information from the Blue Mountains Visitor Centre at Echo Point. The distance above is for the red route marked on the map.

Before Sydneysiders discovered the beach, they went to the mountains. In the 1920s, the city's well-to-do retreated from the scorching city summers to the cool mountain air, creating a series of attractive townships full of guesthouses and cafes serving classic Devonshire teas. Today's visitors tend to be more adventurous, exploring the pockets of rainforest, ferns and hanging swamps, as well as the vast forests of eucalypts, which breath their oil into the air, giving the mountains their eponymous haze.

Rugged playground

The mountains here are not particularly tall; Mount Victoria, the highest point, is a mere 1,111 metres (3,645ft) above sea level. However, the terrain is so rugged that it can hide an entire species of tree (the Wollemi pine) that was thought to have been extinct for 150 million years before it was recently rediscovered. The terrain has hidden the odd ill-prepared explorer too, as young British backpacker Jamie Neale found out in 2009, when he narrowly escaped death after going missing for 12 days, having apparently ventured out for a day walk.

Early convicts apparently believed that China lay on the other side of the mountains, but since they were considered virtually impassable, the authorities weren't too concerned

The spectacular range   *Wentworth Falls*

about a mass escape in that direction. (Although, it's possible a former convict called John Wilson, who lived with the Aborigines after being released in 1792 and claimed to have gone beyond the mountains, may indeed have been the first European to achieve a crossing – his descriptions later turned out to have a ring of truth about them.)

But it wasn't only the convicts that were prone to obsessing about greener fields. Crossing the mountains to access the lush pastures on the western side was one of the greatest challenges facing the early colonists. Indigenous tribes had of course been crossing from the inland to the coast for thousands of years, but since no one thought to ask them for advice, it was not until 1813 that explorers Blaxland, Lawson and Wentworth managed the feat. Today's Great Western Highway closely follows the route they took, as does the railway that provides easy access between the city and the mountains for a growing number of commuters and weekend adventurers.

The mountains' rugged landscape makes it the perfect destination for thrill seekers. Abseiling, canyoning, rock climbing and mountain biking are all popular activities, and offer a unique way to experience this wilderness. Reputable companies include **High n Wild Mountain Adventures** (www.high-n-wild.com.au).

The Blue Mountains World Heritage Area is also home to around 400 species of birds, reptiles and mammals, 40 of which are listed as rare or endangered.

LEAVING SYDNEY

The Blue Mountains may be one of Sydney's most scenic destinations, but the drive there is anything but. To reach the Great Western Highway that takes you into the hills, head west on Parramatta Road from

Waterfall near Leura

the city centre, then follow the signs. Depending on traffic, it will take you about 90 minutes to clear the urban sprawl and start heading up through the lower mountains townships such as Springwood and Faulconbridge, where the scenery slowly starts to change to classic wooded mountain landscape.

NORMAN LINDSAY GALLERY AND MUSEUM

If you feel you need to stretch your legs before you reach Wentworth Falls, you can stop at Faulconbridge to visit the **Norman Lindsay Gallery and Museum ❶** (14 Norman Lindsay Crescent; www.normanlindsay.com.au; daily 10am–4pm; charge), once the home of one of Australia's most notorious artists, who is as famous for his Bacchanalian nudes as he is for his much-loved children's book, *The Magic Pudding*. Lindsay's libertine lifestyle is the subject of the 1993 film *Sirens*, starring Sam Neill, Elle Macpherson, Portia de Rossi, Kate Fischer and Hugh Grant. To reach the gallery, turn right from the Great Western Highway into Grose Road, and follow the signs.

Set in beautifully landscaped gardens, the stone cottage in which Lindsay lived for 57 years, until his death in 1969, now houses a major collection of his work. The 16 hectares (40 acres) of elaborate gardens feature some of his larger statues and fountains, and his studio is set up as if he had just stepped out for a minute.

WENTWORTH FALLS

Return to the Great Western Highways and continue towards the mountains. If you did not stop at the gallery, by the time you reach the township of **Wentworth Falls ❷**, you will be ready for a break. Either turn right into Station Street as you come into town and stop at **Conditorei Patisserie Schwarz**,

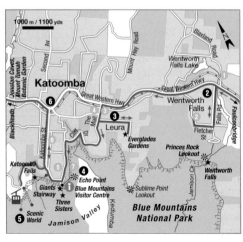

Three women looking at the peaks of the Three Sisters

see ❶, or stay on the Great Western Highway and take the next left at Falls Road (look for the sign to Wentworth Falls National Park). Fletcher Street is the third cross street; turn right at the sign for **The Conservation Hut**, see ❷. The hut is at the end of the street; from here, you can access a variety of viewpoints, including Princes Rock Lookout, which gives a good view of Wentworth Falls. The mountains' best waterfall is impressive when it is in full flood; during dry periods it slows down to a trickle.

LEURA

Head back to the Great Western Highway and continue on to **Leura** ❸, one of the prettiest villages in the mountains. Its main street, The Mall, is peppered with craft studios, antique joints and teashops, and it has one of the area's best restaurants, **Silk's Brasserie**, see ❸. Also on The Mall is **Café Madeleine**, see ❹ – the sister cafe to fine chocolate emporium Josophan's (132 Leura Mall; www.josophans.com.au), so you can get stuck into some fantastic fair-trade chocolate cakes, which are the specialty here.

Green-fingered visitors will love **Everglades Gardens** (37 Everglades Avenue, Leura; www.everglades.org.au; spring and summer daily 10am–5pm, autumn and winter 10am–4pm; charge), which features 5 hectares (12 acres) of landscaped grounds. To get there from Leura Mall, turn left into Craigend Street, then right into Everglades Avenue.

ECHO POINT

Keep driving down The Mall and follow the scenic clifftop drive to Katoomba. On the way you will pass **Solitary Restaurant and Kiosk**, see ❺. Stop at **Echo Point** ❹, where a lookout provides a magnificent view over the famous **Three Sisters** rock formation and into the Jamison Valley. There is also a **Blue Mountains Visitor Centre** (daily 9am–5pm; tel: 1300 653 408) located here.

Scenic World

Several bush walks are accessible from Echo Point. Take the **Giants Stairway** to the left of the Three Sisters, which descends 1,000 steps to the valley floor, from where walks of varying length and difficulty begin. Turn right to take an easy two-hour walk to the **Scenic Railway**, part of **Scenic World** ❺ (Top Station, corner of Violet Street and Cliff Drive, Katoomba; www.scenicworld. com.au; daily 9am–5pm; charge). Originally constructed in the 1880s to transport miners and coal up from the valley, it is the steepest railway incline in the world, and the swift ride up a sheer cliff face at a 45-degree angle can be nerve-racking. If it's any consolation, the ride back down is even more so, providing passengers with the sensation that they're plunging 445 metres (1,460ft) to the valley floor.

Travelling up to the Scenic World Skyway

Alternatively, return to Katoomba via the **Scenic Cableway**, which makes the steep trip to the clifftop. There you will also find the **Scenic World Skyway**, a glass-floored cable car that takes a 720 metre suspended trip across the Jamison Valley, offering unbeatable views.

KATOOMBA

From here, depending on where you have left your car, you can head into the township of **Katoomba** ❹ by taking bus No. 686 from the stop outside Scenic World. Katoomba has a slightly scruffy air, but Katoomba Street has some interesting antiques and new-age shops to browse. Treat yourself to a hot drink in Katoomba's **Cafe Paragon**, see ❻, before strolling back to

The colourful Campbell Rhododendron Garden

Echo Point to pick up the car. If you are in need of more substantial refreshment at this point, visit the highly rated **Darley's**, see ❼.

BLACKHEATH

If you are still feeling energetic, you can explore the next township, **Blackheath** ❼, before checking into your hotel. Originally called Hounslow, this settlement was a favourite stopping place for 19th-century miners heading west to dig for gold. It was renamed by Governor Macquarie in 1815 because of its black, wild look.

Campbell Rhododendron Gardens and Bush Walk

The **Campbell Rhododendron Gardens** (Bacchante Street, Blackheath; www.rhodogarden.org.au; daily 9am–4pm; charge) feature more than 1,500 rhododendrons in a bush setting, and are particularly spectacular from September through to November.

You can also explore a breathtaking **bushwalk** from Govett's Leap lookout to Pulpit Rock, which offers an awe-inspiring panorama. The walk is about 6km (4 miles), but there is an easy option: it is just 400 metres from the car park to the three-level Pulpit Rock lookout, which has a 240-degree view into Govett's Gorge and the Grose Valley.

This should bring you to the end of the first day. Options for staying overnight in Leura include **Broomelea Bed**

A Scenic World Skyway cable car

and Breakfast (see page 107) and in Katoomba, **Echoes and Lialianfels** (see page 107), home to Darley's (see page 93).

JENOLAN CAVES

The following morning, take the Great Western Highway past Mount Victoria and the Victoria Pass. Just after the village of Hartley, the turnoff for Jenolan Caves is on your left. Follow the road all the way to the spectacular **Jenolan Caves ❶** (Jenolan Caves Road, Jenolan; www.jenolancaves.org.au; daily 9.30am–5.30pm; charge). The drive will take about an hour; the last section of the road is very narrow, and must be tackled slowly. Every day between 11.45am and 1.15pm, this final section becomes one-way, to allow coaches to travel safely on the narrow road. That means these hours are also peak visiting time. Plan your visit for early in the day. If necessary, there is an alternate route from the caves, via the Oberon Road.

Jenolan Caves is a mighty series of underground limestone halls encrusted with archways, stalactites, stalagmites and subterranean rivers. Eleven of the caves are open to the public. The caves, known to the Aborigines as Binoomea, or 'dark places', were officially discovered by local farmer James Whalan in 1838. Legend has it that the caves had previously been used as a hideout by the outlaw and bushranger James McKeown, a former convict.

Early finds

The first cave, the Elder Cave, was explored in 1848, but it was not until 1860 that the Lucas Cave, the largest of the show caves, was discovered. In 1866, the caves were brought under government control, and in 1884 the name Jenolan Caves (from the Aboriginal word meaning 'high mountain') was given to the complex that had previously been known as the Binda ('fish river') Caves.

Many of the most spectacular caves – including the River, Temple of Baal, Orient, Ribbon and Pool of Cerberus caves – were discovered during the first years of the 20th century, when explorations were still being done by candlelight. These days the caves boast electric lighting, and some feature multimedia sound-and-light shows. Much of the cave system, which is estimated to extend around 40km (25 miles), remains to be explored; recent discoveries include the Barralong Cave in 1963 and the Spider Cave in 1975.

Cave tours

Tickets for each cave are sold separately, with tours departing every half an hour, occasionally more frequently. Cave tours generally last around 90 minutes, and discounts apply if you visit more than one cave. Among the most popular caves are the Pool of Cerberus Cave and the River Cave – the latter known for its magnificent formations, including spectacular shawls (limestone forma-

Jenolan Caves

tions that hang from a cave's ceiling), stalagmites and columns. The Orient Cave is among the most beautiful, containing three richly coloured chambers, the first of which is wheelchair-accessible. The Imperial Cave is good for the less mobile, and contains the bones of a wallaby and a Tasmanian devil (long extinct on the Australian mainland).

Adventure caving

Those who are looking for an experience with a bit more edge should sign up for one of the adventure tours that let you crawl and climb through caves lit only by your headlamp. The Plughole Tour, for example, starts with a 10-metre abseil into the Elder Cave, and takes in roomy caverns and narrow tunnels before culminating in the Imperial Cave.

MOUNT TOMAH BOTANIC GARDEN

Take Jenolan Caves Road back to the Great Western Highway, and turn right towards Mount Victoria. From Mt Victoria, head north towards the township of Bell, from where you can make a detour to the **Zig Zag Railway** ❾ (see box) by turning left, or reach Mount Tomah Botanic Garden by turning right. **Mount Tomah Botanic Garden** ❿ (Bell's Line of Road; www.rbgsyd.nsw. gov.au; Oct–Mar: daily 10am–5pm, Apr–Sept: 10am–4pm; charge) lies about 20 minutes down the road and is the cool-climate cousin of Sydney's Royal Botanic Gardens (see page 41).

Highlights of the garden, spread over 11 hectares (28 acres), include the Rhododendron Collection and the Gondwana Forest Walk, which showcases the related plant species of the prehistoric super-continent of Gondwana that included Australia, New Zealand, South America and Africa. The walk includes a grove of extremely rare Wollemi pines (fewer than 100 are known to exist in the wild), the ancient species discovered in the Blue Mountains in 1994. The gardens have picnic facilities, including free electric barbecues, and a good restaurant.

From Mount Tomah, return to Sydney via Bells Line of Road to Richmond, from where signs will direct you back to the city.

Zig Zag Railway

Rail buffs will want to take a detour (signposted from Mount Victoria) to the Zig Zag Railway (www.zigzagrailway.com. au), a 13km (8-mile) full-size, narrow-gauge railway that descends the western escarpment of the mountains. It was built in the 1860s and operated until 1910, when a 10-tunnel deviation opened. Sadly, the 2013 New South Wales bushfires caused extensive damage to its structure and rolling stock. At time of press, the Zig Zag Railway was still closed, although its operators hope to resume services as soon as possible. Check the website for updates.

Mount Toombah Botanic Gardens

Food and drink

❶ CONDITOREI PATISSERIE SCHWARZ

30 Station Street, Wentworth Falls;
tel: 4757 3300; daily 7.30am–5.30pm;
$
There is always a crush in this café. Stock
up on terrific rye and sourdough breads, or
authentic German cakes such as poppyseed
strudel. They also offer picnic packs for
bushwalkers.

❷ THE CONSERVATION HUT

Fletcher Street, Wentworth Falls; tel: 4757
3827; www.conservationhut.com.au; daily
9am–4pm; $$
Whether on the terrace in summer or by the
log fire in winter, this is a great place to soak
up the stunning view while enjoying a hearty
meal, with options from pies to pan-roasted
chicken.

❸ SILK'S BRASSERIE

128 The Mall, Leura; tel: 4784 2534;
www.silksleura.com; daily noon–2.30pm &
6pm–9pm; $$–$$$
One of the mountains' most enduring dining
institutions does high-class food without
attitude. Occasional Asian touches enliven
more traditional offerings such as pan-fried
snapper.

❹ CAFÉ MADELEINE

187a The Mall, Leura; tel: 4784 3833; daily
9am–5pm; $
You could order eggs benedict or a smoked

salmon bagel – and don't forget to try the
chocolate cake.

❺ SOLITARY RESTAURANT AND KIOSK

90 Cliff Drive, Leura Falls; tel: 4782 1164;
www.solitary.com.au; Wed–Thu & Sun
11am–4.30pm; Fri–Sat 11am–4.30pm &
6.30pm–late; $–$$$
A weatherboard cottage with panoramic
views of the Jamison Valley, Solitary's kiosk
delivers good-value breakfasts, lunches
and afternoon teas, while the fine-dining
restaurant offers weekend lunches and
dinners. Restaurant bookings essential.

❻ CAFE PARAGON

63–7 Katoomba Street, Katoomba; tel:
4782 2928; Sun–Fri 10am–4pm, Sat
10am–10.30pm; $–$$
The mountain air is often chilly; if you feel the
need to warm up with a cuppa, head straight
for the Paragon, where the gorgeous 1930s Art
Deco interior has been listed by the National
Trust. They also do a killer hot chocolate.

❼ DARLEY'S

Lilianfels Blue Mountains Resort & Spa,
Echo Point, Katoomba; tel: 4780 1200; www.
lilianfels.com.au; Tue–Sat 6pm–10pm; $$$
Hands-down the best meals available in
the mountains, but expect to pay for the
privilege. The small rooms make for an
intimate dining experience – all the better
to savour the sophisticated, seasonal
modern Australian cuisine. Reserve or be
disappointed.

A peaceful beach in the Royal National Park

ROYAL NATIONAL PARK

The world's second-oldest national park covers 16,300 hectares (40,200 acres) of dense bushland, towering coastal cliffs, deep river valleys and pristine beaches, and lies just an hour south of Sydney.

DISTANCE: 26km (16 miles)
TIME: A full day
START/END: Sydney
POINTS TO NOTE: This route is best done by car. To access the park, head south from Sydney's CBD via the Princes Highway, following the signs to Sutherland and Wollongong. The route and the park entrance are well signposted. Pack a picnic lunch; apart from kiosks stocking snacks, there are no food outlets in the park. The distance above is from Audley.

Of all the world's national parks, only Yellowstone in the US is older than Sydney's, which was created in 1879. Far from aiming to preserve the area's natural landscape, the park's founders tried to replicate London's Hampstead Heath, importing plants, rabbits, foxes and deer. Nowadays, the emphasis is firmly on protecting native flora and fauna, and the park has over 150km (90 miles) of walking trails for visitors to enjoy.

AUDLEY

The **Royal National Park Visitor Centre** (Sir Bertram Stevens Drive, Audley; tel: 9542 0648; daily 8.30am–4.30pm) lies 3km (2 miles) inside the park gates. This is a great place to pick up maps and information about the park. Facilities nearby include barbecues, picnic shelters, toilets and a small kiosk. The township of **Audley** ❶ is a popular place with families and you can hire rowing boats, canoes and kayaks from the Audley Boatshed.

INTO THE BUSH

From Audley, continue along Sir Bertram Stevens Drive for about 10 minutes then take the turn off to Wattamolla. En route you will experience some of the park's dramatic bush landscapes, which include towering trees such as eucalypts angophoras, turpentine and blackbutt trees. The park is home to a wide range of fauna, including swamp wallabies, echidnas and marsupial mice. The animals you are most likely to come across, however, are some of the park's 200 species

Driving through the park　　　　　　*Impressive coastal cliffs*

of bird, including honeyeaters and wattlebirds in the shrublands, and sea eagles and the occasional albatross at the coast. If you want to experience waking up to the bush morning chorus, the park has a number of camping sites. Talk to the visitor centre or call 02 9542 0683 (daily 10.30am–1.30pm) for more details.

WATTAMOLLA BEACH

Wattamolla Beach ❷ is one of the park's most popular beaches, thanks to its sheltered lagoon. There are picnic facilities here, and the trees that fringe the lagoon offer plenty of shade. From the car park you can also access a number of walks that form part of the park's 26km (16-mile) Coast Walk.

Head back up Wattamolla Road to rejoin Sir Bertram Stevens Drive heading south. It will take about 15 minutes to reach the turn off for **Garie Beach ❸**, perhaps the park's prettiest beach. Surfers love the rolling breaks.

FOREST PATH

Head back up Garie Road to rejoin Sir Bertram Stevens Drive heading south.

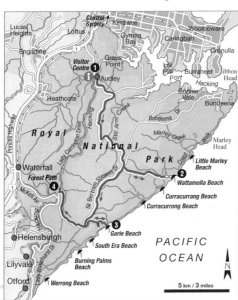

After about 10 minutes, the entrance to Lady Carrington Drive will be on your right. Park here and look for the entrance to the **Forest Path ❹**, just to the left of the drive. This 90-minute looping bushwalk passes through dense pockets of rainforest. If you're very lucky, you may hear a whip bird or spot such spectacular creatures as the lyrebird, or the iridescent plumage of the satin bowerbird.

Just past the Forest Path is McKell Avenue, a turn off to the settlement of Waterfall, which will lead you out of the park. From here, signs indicate the way back to Sydney.

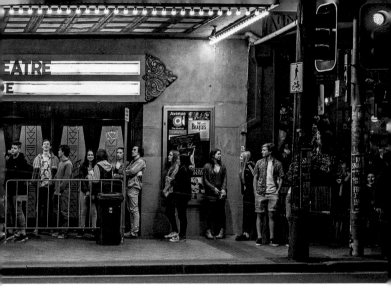

DIRECTORY

Hand-picked hotels and restaurants to suit all budgets and tastes, organised by area, plus select nightlife listings, an alphabetical listing of practical information and an overview of the best books and films to give you a flavour of the city.

Bathroom at the Amora Hotel Jamison Street

ACCOMMODATION

Perhaps surprisingly, you do not have to spend a fortune to sleep well in Sydney. Yes, at the city's most famous hotels, the ones where every window frames its own harbour view, prices can soar into the stratosphere. But in the CBD and districts such as Darling Harbour, there are lots of mid- and budget-priced options. Neighbourhoods such as Potts Point and Darlinghurst are home to some hidden gems that combine central locations with oceans of charm and style.

CBD

Amora Hotel Jamison Street

11 Jamison Street; tel: 9696 2500; www.sydney.amorahotels.com; $$$

While the big names battle it out amongst themselves, the Amora has kept a lower profile, offering its discerning guests a stylish inner-city experience at great rates. All the rooms have marble bathrooms and mod cons including Internet access and computer game consoles, but ask for one with harbour or city views. The hotel's secret weapon is its divine Angsana Day Spa, the perfect place for a bit of pampering.

Australian Heritage Hotel

100 Cumberland Street, The Rocks; tel: 9247 2229; www.australianheritagehotel. com; $

If you like your accommodation served up with a slice of history, this bed and breakfast is the place for you. Housed in a typical Federation-style pub in The Rocks, the location makes it easy to stroll down to the harbour, into the heart of the city, or around Sydney's oldest district. Rooms are tastefully decorated with antiques, and the roof terrace is the perfect place to soak up a harbour view over a cold beer at the end of the day. One word of warning: bathroom facilities are shared.

Base Sydney

477 Kent Street; tel: 9267 7718; www.stayatbase.com; $

Youth hostels are not what they used to be, and nowhere proves this point better than Base. Accommodation ranges from twin rooms to multi-bed dormitories, all of which feature surprisingly stylish furnishings. There are added extras, such as free use of the solarium, personal underbed storage lockers and a women-only floor called The Sanctuary.

Price for a double room for one night without breakfast:
$$$$ = over A$350
$$$ = A$250–350
$$ = A$150–250
$ = below A$150

Harbour view at the Four Seasons

Bed and Breakfast Sydney Harbour

140–142 Cumberland Street, The Rocks, tel: 9247 1130, www.bbsydneyharbour. com.au; $$–$$$

This restored early 20thcentury building is located around the corner from the busiest part of The Rocks, and within a 10-minute walk of Circular Quay. There are nine rooms, some of which have harbour views, are nicely fitted out with period furniture, queen-size beds, and most have their own bathroom. The three-course cooked breakfasts (included in the price) are served in the tree-shaded private courtyard.

Establishment

5 Bridge Lane; tel: 9240 3100; www.merivale.com.au; $$$–$$$$

It would be possible – if expensive – to spend an entire week in Sydney, drinking only at venues owned by the Hemmes family, purveyors of super-slick bars and clubs including those contained in Establishment and The Ivy Bar (see page 121). They also offer accommodation at Establishment: 31 super-chic rooms and two penthouse suites. The decor varies across the rooms, but if you think black timber floorboards and lilac suede daybeds, along with Bulgari toiletries, you are heading in the right direction.

Four Seasons

199 George Street, The Rocks; tel: 9250 3100; www.fourseasons.com/ sydney; $$$–$$$$

Much of Sydney life revolves around attaining a harbour view; check in to the Four Seasons, and that is one thing you will not have to worry about. In addition to sweeping vistas across the harbour, taking in the Opera House and the Botanic Gardens, the Four Seasons offers large rooms tastefully done in neutral tones – plus an outdoor pool.

Fraser Suites

488 Kent Street; tel: 8823 8888; http://sydney.frasershospitality.com; $$$

Sexy is not usually a word applied to serviced apartments, but then, most serviced apartments do not feature a 6-metre (20ft) rainfall chandelier in the lobby. This all-studio complex, designed by internationally renowned architects Foster & Partners (as in Norman Foster – he who designed the new Wembley Stadium), is both sexy and luxurious. There is fine bone china in the kitchens, a huge gym and – bliss – windows that actually open. A wonderful treat.

Harbour Rocks Hotel

34 Harrington Street, tel: 8220-9999, www.harbourrocks.com.au; $$–$$$

This very moderately priced hotel (for The Rocks at least) is a real find. Some of the 55 rooms in this 150-year-old building overlook the harbour (ask for them when booking - you never know your luck). All in all it's a well-appointed and perfectly situated four-star boutique property.

Hilton Hotel

488 George Street; tel: 9266 2000;
www.hiltonsydney.com.au; $$$

If your choice of a hotel hinges upon on how cool its bar or restaurant is, the Hilton is for you. Zeta Bar is a chic spot to savour a drink or two, while the hotel's premier restaurant, Glass Brasserie, is overseen by one of Australia's top chefs, Luke Mangan. Add a central location and sleek, spacious guest rooms, and it's no wonder the Hilton is popular.

Holiday Inn Old Sydney

55 George Street, tel: 9252-0524,
www.holidayinn.com; $$$

A relatively cheap, 174-room option in an absolutely stunning location in the middle of The Rocks, with heated rooftop swimming pool, overlooking the harbour and Opera House, plus a sauna, spa and secure undercover parking. Staff are helpful too. Keep your expectations in check in terms of the rooms – they're functional, not flash – but you can't have everything.

Hotel InterContinental Sydney

117 Macquarie Street; tel: 9253 9000,
www.ichotelsgroup.com; $$$$

Housed in an elegant building that incorporates Sydney's historic Treasury Building, the InterContinental combines 19thcentury grace with 21st-century comfort. Poised on one of the city's stateliest thoroughfares, and within walking distance of the harbour, the Opera House and the Royal Botanic Gardens, this hotel offers a swimming pool, health club and sauna.

The Langham

89–113 Kent Street, The Rocks; tel: 9256 2222; www.langhamhotels.com/en/the-langham/sydney; $$$$

Formerly know as the Observatory Hotel – and still offering an Observatory suite, complete with views of said Observatory – the Langham folks have retained the old-school luxury feel, but given this 96-room 5-star hotel a welcome freshen up. The personal approach has remained too. It boasts a great bar and a fantastic spa, where you can do backstroke in a 20-metre (65ft) pool.

Oaks Hyde Park Plaza

38 College Street; tel: 9331-6933;
www.oakshotelsresorts.com; $$–$$$

In a great position, overlooking the park with Oxford Street just around the corner, this hotel offers a variety of self-contained apartments, ranging from studios to two-bedroom family suites and three-bedroom executive suites. Rooms are generally about twice the size of other hotel rooms. Some have balconies overlooking the park and city. There's also a heated pool, spa, sauna and gym.

Park Hyatt Hotel

7 Hickson Road, The Rocks; tel: 9241 1234; www.sydney.park.hyatt.com; $$$$

A hotel room at the Shangri-La with unbeatable views of Sydney's harbour

They say there are three rules in real estate – location, location, location – and locations do not get better than this. The low-rise sandstone hotel hugs the foreshore smack bang opposite the Opera House. If you really need more convincing, the super-spacious rooms come with butler service and sink-into marble tubs. Guests can also treat themselves to swim in the rooftop pools, or a meal in the acclaimed dining room.

Pensione Hotel Sydney

631–5 George Street; tel: 9265-8888; www.8hotels.com; $$

The rooms here are a bit small, and it is important to note that the noise from the street can be heard in street-facing rooms, but the staff are famous for their friendly attitude and eagerness to make your visit memorable. There is a guest lounge which is a particularly relaxing sitting area with a library and communal kitchenette. The free CBD shuttle stops at the front door.

Rydges World Square

389 Pitt Street; tel: 8268-1888; www.rydges.com; $$–$$$

This hotel 450-room hotel is adjacent to the World Square Shopping Centre, with a Monorail station at the front door. It is highly regarded for its 'green' environmental design and operating standards.

The Russell Hotel

143 George Street; tel: 9241 3543; www.therussell.com.au; $$–$$$

A very comfortable boutique hotel, which takes full advantage of the high ceilings and architecture of the 1887 building – plenty of room for cat swinging here (BYO cat). Furnishings, often antiques, reflect the period. The rooftop garden overlooks the harbour and the street-side balcony looks down upon George Street – scenery versus people watching – everyone's a winner. Most rooms have en suite bathrooms; all have ceiling fans, hairdryers, bathrobes. The rate includes a continental breakfast.

Shangri-La Hotel

176 Cumberland Street, The Rocks; tel: 9250 6000; www.shangri-la.com/sydney; $$$

One of a handful of serious contenders for the title of Sydney's Best Hotel, the Shangri-La still manages to deliver personalised service despite its 500-plus rooms. And it gets better from there. The guest rooms, each of which has a harbour view, are super-sized: the smallest are 40 sq metres (430 sq ft). Guests also enjoy complimentary broadband access, and one of the city's most stunning cocktail bars, Blu Bar on 36 (see page 121).

Sheraton on the Park

161 Elizabeth Street; tel: 9286-6000; http://www.sheratonontheparksydney.com; $$$$

Superior King Room, Sir Stamford at Circular Quay

No harbour views here, but you can gaze out on the verdant foliage of Hyde Park from the upper floors of this 500-plus room five-star hotel. Rooms and surrounds boast slick and contemporary decor, and the grand lobby and sweeping staircases are complemented by a modern health club and gym. It is conveniently located near Sydney's prime shopping venues and department stores.

Sir Stamford at Circular Quay

93 Macquarie Street; tel: 9252 4600; www.stamford.com.au; $$$–$$$$

Sensational service in a very elegant and upscale hotel, filled with oil paintings, Persian rugs and similar clubby trappings. It's a little bit away from the hustling and bustling heart of The Rocks, but still within easy striking distance, and even closer to the Royal Botanic Gardens, which are right opposite.

Sydney Central YHA

Pitt Street and Rawson Place; tel: 9218-9000; www.yha.com.au; $–$$

Technically a youth hostel, this is also an excellent, centrally located hotel in a heritage building opposite Central Station. Most rooms are dormitory-style: they are comfortable, but you will be rooming with strangers and sharing a bathroom. However, they are cheap, safe and clean. Private rooms are pricier, but still good value. The YHA also has a pool, sauna, laundry and self-catering kitchens.

Y Hotel Hyde Park

5-11 Wentworth Ave; tel: 9264 2451; www.yhotels.com.au; $-$$

A good, clean, super centrally located B&B option, offering no-thrills by very functional rooms at very affordable prices in a peach of a location, right next to Sydney's Hyde Park. Also close to a plethora of restaurants, bars and attractions. Book direct to get free wifi and breakfast.

YHA, The Rocks

110 Cumberland Street, tel: 8272-0900, www.yha.com.au; $–$$

An excellent option for travelling families (family rooms for up to six people are available) and anyone on a budget, the YHA offers one of the best locations in Sydney for a fraction of the price that you'll pay in any of the luxury hotels that are just a stone's throw away. Some rooms even have harbour views. All rooms are safe and comfortable, and there's a mixture of shared and private rooms.

Darling Harbour and around

APX Apartments Darling Harbour

8 Dixon Street, Darling Harbour; tel: 8281 4700; www.apxhotelsapartments.com/darlingharbour; $–$$

Comfortable, furnished apartments in both studio and one-bedroom layouts – some with private balconies – make this Dixon Street address another popular choice with families. There's free wi-fi, and travelling gourmets may also

Exterior of the Vulcan Hotel

like to consider this hotel for its proximity to a wide array of won't-break-the-bank dining options. Darling Harbour, Cockle Bay and Liverpool Street's Spanish quarter are all nearby, but best of all are the many mouth-watering eateries of Chinatown.

Four Points by Sheraton

161 Sussex Street; tel: 9290 4000, www.starwoodhotels.com/fourpoints; $$$–$$$$

Welcome to the whopper – the largest hotel in all of Australia. Although this is a bit of a big Tardis – the elegant, curved face that it presents to Darling Harbour belies its size (648 rooms, including 17 suites). If you can find your way out of it, the Four Points is a short walk or Monorail ride from the CBD and Sydney entertainment venues.

Novotel Rockford Darling Harbour

17 Little Pier Street, Darling Harbour; tel: 8217 4000; www.accorhotels.com; $$$

Another great Sydney hotel for families. The rooms themselves are bright, spacious and airy, and the pool is an excellent way for kids to burn off excess energy. The location is also close to key family attractions such as Sydney Aquarium, the Powerhouse Museum and everything else Darling Harbour has to offer.

Oaks Goldsbrough Apartments

243 Pyrmont Street, Darling Harbour; tel:

8586 2500; www.theoaksgroup.com.au; $–$$

The Goldsbrough Apartments offer the best of both worlds: sleek, modern interiors, set in a historic building dating back to 1883. The lovely neo-classical facade hides a property where airy dimensions, local hardwood floors and exposed columns add a romantic ambience to the selection of studios, one- and two-bedroom apartments. Fitness fans are catered for with a lap pool, spa, sauna and gymnasium.

Vulcan Hotel

500 Wattle Street, Ultimo; tel: 9211 3283; www.vulcanhotel.com.au; $–$$

The stylish Vulcan Hotel is one of Sydney's hidden gems – quite an achievement for a hotel that first started welcoming guests back in 1894. Located in a National Heritage-listed building close to Darling Harbour, this boutique hotel's 46 rooms include doubles, triples and studios in a variety of configurations. The interiors, including the private landscaped courtyard, offer oodles of urban chic, and the service is both intimate and friendly. Highly recommended.

Woolbrokers Hotel

22 Allen Street, Pyrmont; tel: 9552 4773, www.woolbrokershotel.com.au; $$

Very basic, but very central, two-star B&B-style hotel in the heart of Darling Harbour. No air-conditioning or lift, and most of the rooms share a bathroom,

Room at the Vibe Hotel Rushcutters

but staff are friendly and it's in a fantastic location. If you're on a budget, the price and the position make this a great option.

Potts Point and around

Bayview Boulevard Sydney

90 William Street, Woolloomooloo; tel: 1800 671 222; www.bayviewhotels.com; $$

This old Sydney stalwart was fully renovated a few years ago, and now offers many of the benefits of the best hotels in town, without the price tag. Many of the rooms have stunning harbour and city views, and feature mod cons such as free Internet access. The location is also terrific, just 15 minutes' walk from the heart of town and the hip spots of Darlinghurst. Great for both business and leisure travellers.

Blue Sydney

6 Cowper Wharf Road, Woolloomooloo; tel: 9331 9000; www.bluehotel.com.au; $$$

There is a lot to love about this hotel located in one of Sydney's historic timber wharves. The rooms are stylish; the hotel's bars are buzzing; some of Sydney's best restaurants are on your doorstep. Then there's the waterside location, and the service. Some of the rooms are on the small side, but who spends a lot of time in their room in Sydney?

De Vere Hotel

44–46 Macleay Street, Potts Point; tel: 9358-1211, www.devere.com.au; $–$$

A good, comfortable budget choice in the heart of the Potts Point and Kings Cross entertainment district, and still close to city attractions. Some rooms on upper floors have harbour views. With 100 rooms available, there's a wide range of options, from budget single to family studios.

Hotel 59

59 Bayswater Road, Rushcutters Bay; tel: 9360 5900; www.hotel59.com.au; $

Located in a quiet section of Bayswater Road, this small hotel offers just nine cheerful, spotlessly clean, no-frills rooms and self-catering family accommodation. Excellent cooked breakfasts are included in the price.

Vibe Hotel

100 Bayswater Road, Rushcutters Bay; tel: 8353 8988; www.vibehotels.com.au; $$

There are a number of Vibe Hotels in Sydney, but location-wise, this is the pick of the bunch, with a bayside setting close to the hip neighbourhoods of Darlinghurst and Potts Point, and not far from the city centre. Vibe takes a fresh, friendly approach, updating standard hotel rooms with a funky flair while still offering all the amenities and services that you would expect.

Victoria Court Sydney

122 Victoria Street, Potts Point; tel: 9357-3200, www.victoriacourt.com.au; $–$$

Located in a building that dates back to 1881 and is situated on a quiet, leafy street in Potts Point, this B&B has bucketloads of charm. Depending on which of the 22 rooms you get, you may have a marble fireplace, balcony or four-poster bed. All of the rooms have en suite bathrooms and there are loads of good cafés and restaurants nearby.

Darlinghurst and Surry Hills

57 Hotel

57 Foveaux Street, Surry Hills; tel: 9011 5757; www.57hotel.com.au; $$
A cool and modern boutique hotel in a cracking location, close to Central Station and within striking distance of all Sydney's major attractions. Some rooms include bathrooms with tinted glass walls, providing a view of the urbanscape, even while you wash the gritty city from your pores.

Cambridge Hotel

212 Riley Street, Surry Hills; tel: 9212 1111; www.cambridgehotel.com.au; $$
Basic, but eminently serviceable and well-located, close to cafés, bars, restaurants and Museum Station. Guests enjoy access to a swimming pool and gym. Go for the rooms on the higher floors for the best views, and facing away from the road to cut down on potential traffic noise. Book direct to get gratis wifi.

City Crown Motel

289 Crown Street, Surry Hills; tel: 9331-2433; www.citycrownmotel.com.au; $$
A very trim, pleasant, family-run property in a trendy street in inner-city Surry Hills, a short stroll from Oxford Street, with plenty of cafés and restaurants around. All 30 rooms have their own bathroom and balcony.

Kirketon Hotel

229 Darlinghurst Road, Darlinghurst; tel: 9332 2011; www.kirketon.com.au; $$
Tucked away in the bosom of Darlinghurst, this slick 40-room boutique hotel is ideally located for Sydney's café, restaurant and bar district. Rooms are fairly small, but the attention to details is ace, and this is a good base for exploring the area. Be aware: there is no lift (but some of the rooms are on the ground floor).

Medusa

267 Darlinghurst Rd, Darlinghurst; tel: 9331 1000; www.medusa.com.au; $$$
One of the coolest boutique bunkhouses in town. If your plans for your Sydney visit involve plenty of late-night clubbing and lots of shopping, Medusa is where you will want to stay. It boasts a central location on funky Darlinghurst Road; a decor that is heavy on big, bold colours; plushly upholstered furniture; and free gym membership for every guest. This all draws a chic crowd that, according to rumour, includes Kylie Minogue. With just 18 rooms, the Medusa offers an intimate welcome that also extends to guests who bring their dogs with them.

Adina Apartment Hotel Bondi Beach

Paddington and Woollahra

Arts Hotel

21 Oxford Street, Paddington; tel: 8599 7154; www.artshotel.com.au; $$

The rooms available at this compact boutique hotel range from standard to 'garden' (facing out onto a quiet courtyard) and 'art' (where flourishes include hypoallergenic bedding, rainshowers, deep pile carpeting and l'Occitane en Provence toiletries). All rooms have free wifi. Clean and quiet, this is handy for all of Paddington's many attractions.

The Hughenden

14 Queen Street, Woollahra; tel: 9363 4863; http://thehughenden.com.au; $$–$$$

Plenty of Sydneysiders fantasise about living in one of the grand mansions lining Woollahra's leafy streets: a stay at The Hughenden lets you try the fantasy on for size. Housed in an Italianite mansion dating back to 1876, the hotel is run by a pair of creative sisters (one a painter, one a writer), who create a welcoming atmosphere that includes afternoon tea in the lobby. The building has quite a history – once owned by the son of Australia's philosopher and Professor of Divinity, Barzillai Quaife, it's been a Masonic Hall, nurses' home and dance hall – so there's plenty to talk about.

Bondi

Adina Apartment Hotel Bondi Beach

69-73 Hall Street; tel: 9300 4800; www.tfehotels.com; $$

Located right on the cusp of Bondi's hip strip, within easy walking distance of the world famous beach itself, these classy studios and one-, two- and three-bedroom apartments are fantastic value. Super spacious, they come with wireless and broadband internet connection, iPod docking facilities and everything else you're going to need, plus a few things you won't – like in-room movies (too much to do just outside the door).

Dive Hotel

234 Arden Street, Coogee; tel: 9665 5538; www.divehotel.com.au; $$

Interesting choice of name for a hotel, but this well-run boutique little place is anything but a dive. Fresh, clean rooms and friendly staff top off a fantastic location, close to Sydney's best beaches and in the thick of the Randwick action, with all the bars and entertainment option that carries with it. Free breakfasts.

Hotel Bondi

178 Campbell Parade, Bondi Beach; tel: 9130 3271, www.hotelbondi.com.au; $–$$

The closest hotel to the beach has been a Bondi landmark for almost 100 years. Its oceanfront rooms have breathtaking views and it's surrounded by shops and restaurants. What's not to like?

Ravesis

Campbell Parade, Bondi Beach; tel: 9365

A shady pool at Adina Apartment Hotel Bondi Beach

4422; www.ravesis.com.au; $$$

Now this is the way to do Bondi. A prime beachside location. An intimate atmosphere, with just 12 sleek, light-filled rooms. Your own balcony, complimentary Wi-Fi, and an in-house bar and restaurant. And in less than five minutes, you can be plunging into the surf. Perfect.

North Shore

Glenferrie Lodge Hotel

12A Carabella Street, Kirribilli; tel: 9955 1685, www.glenferrielodge.com; $–$$

What a difference a harbour makes. The six-minute ferry jaunt from Circular Quay to Kirribilli earns you a room with a balcony overlooking the Opera House, Bridge and Quay at about a quarter of the price of rooms on the other side of the harbour. This place is consistently voted one of the best budget deals in Sydney. The 70 rooms are simple and comfortable, and all share bathrooms. Staff are very friendly and there's a hot breakfast buffet every morning.

Quest Manly

54A West Esplanade, Manly; tel: 9976 4600; www.questmanly.com.au; $$

Fantastic, modern rooms, handy for the ferry and all pubs, restaurants and conveniences, and with two beaches within striking distance of the front door. Winner. Free wifi too. Bit of street noise from the front, depending on what nights you're staying and how lively the locals are feeling.

Blue Mountains

Broomelea Bed and Breakfast

273 Leura Mall, Leura; tel: 4784 2940; www.broomelea.com.au; $$

This gorgeous Federation-style bed and breakfast is nestled in leafy surrounds just a short stroll away from Leura's shops. The cosy rooms have four-poster beds and fireplaces, and the guest lounge is a lovely place to relax after dinner.

Echoes

3 Lilianfels Avenue, Katoomba; tel: 4782 1966; www.echoeshotel.com.au; $$$$

With just 12 rooms, two suites – all individually designed – and a private spa and sauna, this boutique hotel is like having your own amazing holiday house that comes complete with jaw-dropping views of the Jamison Valley. A pre-dinner drink in the glamorous bar or on the terrace is an absolute must.

Lilianfels

Lilianfels Blue Mountains Resort & Spa, Echo Point, Katoomba; tel: 4780 1200; www.lilianfels.com.au; $$$$

The ultimate Blue Mountains retreat, set in a historic country house amid 1 hectare (2.5 acres) of manicured gardens. Lilianfels has an indulgent spa, a superb fine-dining restaurant, and is just 10 minutes' walk from the Three Sisters. Bliss.

Dining with a view at Altitude

RESTAURANTS

Whether you are in the mood for world-class fine dining, super-fresh seafood by the ocean or a cheap and cheerful feast, you will find myriad options in Sydney. The city's chefs work with a wide range of cuisines, so you are as likely to find Asian flavours served up in a five-star dining room as in a hole-in-the-wall diner.

Sydneysiders have a reputation for being fickle foodies, and it is true that the list of hottest dining spots in town changes with tedious regularity. However, there is enough loyalty to ensure the best restaurants in town remain busy most nights of the week. If you are planning a meal in a top restaurant, or one anywhere near the water, it is always advisable to book ahead.

No single suburb of Sydney can claim to be the city's main dining precinct; eateries are scattered throughout the inner city, although it is a fairly good bet that if you find a nice bit of waterfront, there will be a couple of quality restaurants nearby. Darlinghurst and Surry Hills offer a particularly

impressive array of dining options to suit every budget.

CBD

Altitude

Atop the Shangri-La Hotel, 176 Cumberland Street; tel: 9250 6123, www.36levelsabove. com.au/altitude; Mon–Sat 6pm–10pm; $$$$

There is no better view of the city than from the floor-to-ceiling windows at this award-winning restaurant on the 36th floor, although it comes at a price that has altitude as well. If the menu looks a bit steep, enjoy the view from Blu Bar instead.

Bistro Papillon

98 Clarence Street; tel: 9262 2402; www.bistropapillon.com.au; Mon–Fri noon–2.30pm, Sat 6pm–late $$

A classy, welcoming bistro with true French country cuisine, with revolving regional specialities from all over the country, including escargot. The set menus for lunch and dinner are good value.

Din Tai Fung

World Square Shopping Centre, 644 George Street; tel: 9264 6010; www.dintaifung.com. au; daily 11.30am–2.30pm & 5.30pm–9pm, until 10pm Thu–Sat; $

Dumpling heaven. This Taiwanese chain has outlets all over the world, and all

Price for a two-course meal for one person with a glass of house wine:
$$$$ = over A$90
$$$ = $70–90
$$ = A$50–70
$ = below A$50

The Governors Table

over the world you will find diners queuing out the door day and night. The Sydney outlet is no exception. The massive menu offers a bewildering array of dumplings, but ignore the soup dumplings – thin-skinned, juicy morsels filled with pork and broth – at your peril. A total taste sensation...

Encasa

423 Pitt Street, tel: 9211 4257, www.encasa.com.au; Mon–Fri noon–2.30pm & 5.30pm–late, Sat noon–late; $–$$

A well-liked super Spanish restaurant with excellent specials. The paella is tasty and authentic – it takes 45 minutes to prepare, but is well worth the wait.

est.

252 George Street; tel: 9240 3010; www.merivale.com.au/establishmentbar; Mon–Fri 11am–late, from noon Sat–Sun; $$$$

The establishment – est. to its mates – represents a meeting of the minds of two compelling Sydney characters. On the one hand, the king of wining and dining, owner Justin Hemmes provides the elegant dining room in his Establishment complex; on the other, Peter Doyle, who delivers the superb Modern Australian food such as steamed coral trout fillet on shaved abalone. Dining options range from good-value fixed-price lunches to the full tasting menu delight.

The Governors Table

Corner Phillip & Bridge Streets; tel: 9241 178; www.thegovernorstable.com.au; Sat 8.30am–late, Sun 8.30am–3pm, Mon–Fri 12pm–3pm & 5.30pm–late; $$$

This classy restaurant hangs out in the Museum of Sydney and therefore claims a heritage going back to 1788 through right of association. Either way, both its modern cuisine and its setting are stunning, and the Prix Fixe Menu is perfect for post museum recovery or pre-theatre dining.

Hyde Park Barracks Café

Queens Square, Macquarie Street, tel: 9223 1815, www.hydeparkbarrackscafe.com.au; Mon–Fri 8am–3pm, Sat-Sun 9am–3pm; $–$$

Attention! Located in World Heritage-listed convict-built barracks, breakfast here goes well beyond gruel. Tuck into tea, hot meals and smoothies, and enjoy more substantial dishes at lunchtime.

Lindt Chocolat Café

103 Cockle Bay Wharf, Darling Harbour; tel: 9267 8064; Sun–Thur 10am–10pm, Fri-Sat 10am–midnight; $

Chocolate pastries, cakes, ice creams and confections, and a view of the water, make this café the perfect place to get a quick sugar fix when your energy is flagging.

Lord Nelson Brewery Hotel

19 Kent Street, The Rocks; tel: 9251

Tuck in at Sailor's Thai Canteen

4044; www.lordnelsonbrewery.com; Thu–Sat noon–3pm & 6pm–10pm, Tue–Wed 6pm–10pm; $$

The Lord Nelson is a cracking boozer, but the first-floor brasserie serves a blinding meal too, alongside an in-depth wine list. Stars of the innovative menu include sage and beef rigatoni, confit of rabbit legs with star anise.

Medusa Greek Taverna

2 Market Street; tel: 9267 0799; www.medusagreektaverna.com.au; Mon–Fri noon–3pm & 5.30pm–9pm, Sat 5.30pm–9pm; $$

A great place for lovers of authentic, creative Greek cuisine. The contemporary setting accommodates groups of four or more, and you can tuck into a gorgeous Greek banquet, served family-style.

Phillip's Foote

101 George Street, the Rocks; www.phillipsfoote.com.au; tel: 9241 1485; Mon–Sat noon–midnight, Sun noon–10pm; $$

Throw another shrimp on the barbie at this centrally located, legendary Aussie eating house, where you can choose a cut of meat and cook it to your liking on the central grilling station, while piling a plate high with all sorts of great side salads. The restaurant is located in a classy heritage house, has a good wine list, and the atmosphere around the barbeque is always friendly.

Prime

GPO, 1 Martin Place; tel: 9229 7777; www.gpogrand.com; Tue–Fri noon–3pm & 6pm–10pm, no lunch on Mon; $$$–$$$$

When only meat will do, head for Prime. Nestled amid the sandstone arches in the basement of the historic GPO, the feel is gentleman's club, and the menu is aimed at carnivorous connoisseurs, detailing not just cuts but also breeds and ageing details. A treat for beefy boys and Wagyu women.

Sailor's Thai Canteen

106 George Street, The Rocks; tel: 9251 2466; www.sailorsthai.com.au; daily noon–10pm; $$

Thai 'street food' is served in the canteen upstairs, or you can try more formal dishes in the restaurant. The no-nonsense fare is authentic and delicious, served briskly in what used to be a sailor's home. For top views, ask for a table on the balcony.

Spice Temple

10 Bligh Street; tel: 8078 1888; www.rockpool.com/spicetemplesydney; Yum Cha, Mon–Fri noon–3pm; dinner, Mon–Sat 6pm–late; $$–$$$

Globally acclaimed chef Neil Perry has opened (and closed) a number of venues over the years. He kicked 2009 off with a bang, opening two new restaurants in his Bligh Street premises: the relaxed Rockpool Bar and Grill and, in the basement, the atmospheric Spice Temple. The cui-

Seafood is a local speciality

A refreshing dessert, just right for the summer

sine here is Chinese, but not as you know it: Perry revels in the hot and tangy flavours of lesser-known provinces such as Hunan, Jiangxi and Xinjiang. A real treat for those with adventurous tastebuds.

Steel Bar and Grill

60 Carrington Street; tel: 9299 9997; www.steelbarandgrill.com; Mon–Sat noon–3pm & 6pm–late; $$

There's an airy terrace, a flash interior heavy on industrial chic (the loos are a must-visit), and cool staff. However, these aren't the only reasons that Steel is packed out at lunchtimes and after work. The food lives up to its surroundings and has something to appeal to every palate, from a Goan fish curry to salmon and steak.

Tetsuya's

529 Kent Street; tel: 9267 2900; www.tetsuyas.com; Tue–Fri: 5.30pm–late, Sat noon–3pm & 6.30pm–late; $$$$

If you are serious about your food, you cannot leave town with eating at Tetsuya's. And if you are eating at Tet's, you can't not have the 10-course *dégustation* – because it is the only thing on the menu. The combination of Japanese and French influences makes each course an exquisite experience. Remember to book well in advance.

Wine Odyssey

39–43 Argyle Street, The Rocks; tel: 8114 0256; www.wineodyssey.com.au; Tue–Sat noon–late, Sun noon–10pm; $$

Mod Australian cuisine and vegetarian dishes are offered in this restaurant's chic setting. Wine and food flights start at AU$32 for three dishes with three wines. It also offers 'introduction to wine tasting' afternoons.

Opera House and around

Cafe Sydney

5th Floor, Customs House, 31 Alfred Street, Circular Quay; tel: 9251 8683; www.cafesydney.com; Mon–Fri noon–late, Sat 5pm–late, Sun noon–2.30pm; $$$

Found on the fifth floor of Customs House, this is a great spot for a drink with a properly iconic view (cracking cocktails) or an expensive but exquisite meal. Seafood is chef James Kidman's speciality, with rock and pacific oysters, Morton Bay bugs, Coffin Bay octopus and Cone Bay barramundi all starring on the seasonally focused menu. There's live jazz on Sundays.

Bennelong

Sydney Opera House, Bennelong Point; tel: 9241 1999; www.bennelong.com.au; Fri–Sun noon–2pm & 5.30pm–10pm, Mon–Thu 6.30pm–10pm; $$$$

Every visitor to Sydney gawps at the Opera House's shining exterior, but a seat at the table in Bennelong restaurant inside is a hot ticket indeed. Celebrated chef Peter Gilmore has just taken up residence in Guillaume Brahimi's old stomping ground, and the menu is now more Australian than French flavoured. If your budget can't get you through the

door, go for post-theatre tapas in the upstairs bar instead.

China Doll

6 Cowper Wharf Road, Woolloomooloo; tel: 9380 6744; www.chinadoll.com.au; daily noon–2.30pm & 6pm–late; $$$

Sydney offers a cornucopia of Asian foods, from Thai to Laotian, Korean to Vietnamese. If you cannot decide which one you feel like tonight, head for China Doll, where the menu reflects influences from all over the continent. Dishes such as tea-smoked ocean trout, and a prime location on the Finger Wharf, draw in the crowds despite the hefty prices.

Darling Harbour, China Town and Glebe

Badde Manors Café

37 Glebe Point Road, Glebe, tel: 9660-3797, www.baddemanorscafe.com; Sun–Thu 6.30am–midnight, Fri 6.30am–1am, Sat 6.30am–1am; $

Fantastic, internationally inspired, healthy vegetarian food is sold to a funky multicultural crowd throughout the day at this long-established café that has a great atmosphere (to go along with the superb name). Smoothies, cakes, tanjine breakfasts and Badde Manors own veggie shepherd's pie are all amazing (and cheap).

BBQ King

18 Goulburn Street; tel: 9267 2586; until late; $

Never judge a book by its cover, nor a Chinese restaurant by its frontage – judge it by the queues outside. While BBQ King is nearly legendary for its duck and pork dishes, its decor is non-existent. When the food is this good and this fresh, who cares? Try the hot and sour soup, a delicate mélange of flavours.

Golden Century

393–9 Sussex Street, Chinatown; tel: 02 9212 3901; www.goldencentury.com.au; daily noon–4am; $–$$

This is Chinatown at its most authentic: a vast 600-seater restaurant that is packed all hours of the day and late into the night, complete with gold wallpaper, a menu the size of an airport novel, and waiters carrying still-flapping seafood fresh from the tank. People either love it or hate it. Daily specials tend to offer more adventurous choices, while the less daring can stick with favourites like hotpot or crispy-skinned chicken.

The Malaya

King Street Wharf, 39 Lime Street; tel: 02 9279 1170; www.themalaya.com.au; Daily noon–late, no lunch on Sun; $$

Well into its fourth decade, this old favourite has had a makeover, moving into a glamorous new home. Fortunately, although the decor has changed, the food has not. The Malaya still dishes up a broad range of Malay-

Alfresco dining at Aki's

...sian favourites, with the emphasis on the *nonya* cuisine of the country's mixed Malay-Chinese community. If you love flavours of lemongrass, chilli, coconut and tamarind, this is the place for you.

The Thievery

...1 Glebe Point Road, Glebe; tel: 8283 ...329; www.thethievery.com.au; Tue–Thu 6pm–11pm, Fri 6pm–midnight, Sat noon–3pm & 6pm–midnight; $

Experience traditional Lebanese with a contemporary twist here, by getting your chops around the bastourma cigars (halloumi and fermented chilli) or the Lebanese fried chicken with squid-ink, with a side of smbaba ghanoush, served in funky fit-out, where you eat off a door and there are holes in the ceiling. Or just go for a classic lamb kebab – up to you, it's all good.

Potts Point and around

Aki's

...Cowper Wharf Road, Woolloomooloo; ...el: 9332-4600; www.akisindian.com.au; Sun–Fri noon–3pm, daily 6pm–10pm; $

One of the best authentic Indian restaurants in the city, with chef Kumar Mahadevan presenting a menu bursting with flavoursome dishes from various regions of India. Set meals for four or more people cost about AU$55–75 per person, depending on the menu. Aim for a table outside for harbour views.

Billy Kwong

Shop 1, 28 Macleay Street, Potts Point; tel: 9332 3300; www.billykwong.com.au; Mon–Thu 5.30pm–10pm, Fri–Sat 5.30pm–11pm, Sun 5.30pm–9pm; $$–$$$

After 14 massive game-changing years on Crown Street, Kylie Kwong has upped woks and moved Billy to a new (bigger) pad in Potts Point. The food, however, such as the excellent crispy-skin duck with fresh blood-orange sauce and lamb with plum sauce, has remained in situ – anchored in the realm of utterly awesome.

Cafe Sopra

81 Macleay Street, Potts Point; tel: 9368 6655; www.fratellifresh.com.au; Mon–Fri 10am–8pm, Sat–Sun 10am–7pm; $$

Dining surrounded by boxes of leeks or large tins of olive oil may not be everyone's taste, but there's a reason that Fratelli Fresh – a provedore with its own in-house restaurant, Cafe Sopra – is always packed, and that's the mouthwatering menu of rustic, and reasonably priced Italian dishes made from the best seasonal produce.

Fratelli Paradiso

12 Challis Avenue, Potts Point; tel: 9357 1744; www.fratelliparadiso.com; Mon–Sat 7am–11pm, Sun 7am–10pm; $$

Challis Avenue is the heart of Potts Point's cafe society, lined with intimate eateries of every description. Whether Sunday brunch or Thursday night din-

Fish and chips, Sydney-style

ner, Fratelli Paradiso always has a couple of locals queued outside. They succeed by keeping it simple: offering a small selection of creatively updated Italian classics, including a couple of homemade pasta dishes.

Gazebo Wine Garden

2 Elizabeth Bay Road, Elizabeth Bay; tel: 9357 5333; http://love.thegazebo.com.au; Tue–Sun noon–late; $$

There is nothing one-dimensional about the Gazebo. Indoor/outdoor, wine bar/restaurant, classy/quirky (yes, that is a stuffed fox hanging from the ceiling), it is a great place to drop by at any time of the day or well into the night. The friendly staff will happily help you choose a drop from the impressive wine list to wash down the classic bistro fare.

Old Fitzroy Hotel

129 Dowling Street, Woolloomooloo; tel: 9356 3848; www.oldfitzroy.com.au; daily noon-late; $–$$

As befits a working-class suburb, Woolloomooloo has more than its fair share of pubs, but perhaps the best value is the Old Fitzroy Hotel, which has its own studio theatre hosting a range of fringe productions. The combined beer, laksa and theatre ticket offers Sydney's best-value night out.

Darlinghurst, Surry Hills and Paddington

Bill's

433 Liverpool Street, Darlinghurst, tel: 02 9360-9631, www.bills.com.au; Mon-Fri 7am–10pm, Sat-Sun 7.30am–10pm; $–$$

This legendary local-feel café-restaurant serves excellent value breakfasts lunches and dinners, cooked up (or at least dreamt up) by fun-loving foodie Bill Granger. Signature dishes include ricotta hotcakes with honeycomb butter. It's very busy at weekends. Now has sister restaurants in Bondi and Surry Hills (not to mention London, Tokyo, Honolulu and Seoul).

Bodega

216 Commonwealth Street, Surry Hills; tel: 9212 7766; www.bodegatapas.com; Tue-Sat 6pm–late, Fri from noon; $$–$$$

Bodega offers the complete package: funky surroundings, cool waitstaff, and an inviting tapas menu that makes it hard to say 'enough'. Their take on fish fingers – sashimi kingfish on garlic toast with cuttlefish and *mojama* – is a perfect blend of contrasting textures, while more daring combinations, such as seared scallops with pickled Wagyu tongue, also delight. The house tortilla remains the *pièce de résistance*.

Cowbell 808

616 Bourke Street, Surry Hills; tel: 9698 5044; www.cowbell808.com.au; Mon–Sat 7am–3.30pm, Sun 8am–3.30pm; $

Great food (burgers and toasties – but all with a twist of class) and fantastic atmosphere, wrapped up in a noisy

All set for a stylish dinner

backdrop of 80s tunes and 70s decor. Sip an excellent coffee and watch Surry Hill sideshow slide by.

Erciyes

409 Cleveland Street, Surry Hills; tel: 9319 1309; www.erciyesrestaurant.com.au; 11am–midnight; $–$$

Cheap, cheerful and well-patronised Turkish restaurant specialising in *pide* (Turkish pizza). Reservations are recommended at weekends, when belly dancers perform. There's a AU$40 per person banquet deal at weekends.

Fatima's Lebanese Restaurant

294–296 Cleveland Street, Surry Hills; tel: 9698 4895; www.fatimas.com.au; daily 9am–late; $

This was one of Australia's first Lebanese restaurants, and for over 40 years Fatima's has been serving delicious authentic cuisine to Surry Hills' locals. The ambience is great, and the menu boasts an eclectic selection of meaty and veggie options – all priced very reasonably (you can try an 8-course banquet and still pay less than A$30 per person). It even comes complete with cushion room and a live belly dancing show every Friday and Saturday night.

Guillaume

92 Hargrave Street, Paddington; tel: 9302 5222; www.guillaumes.com.au; Fri–Sat noon–late, Tue–Sat 5.45pm–late; $$$$

Prised from his Sydney Opera House shell after many years of thrilling theatre goers with his fabulous French cuisine, Guillaume Brahimi has set up a new restaurant in the leafy streets of Paddington, from where he continues to work wonders. The 8-course degustation menu here is extraordinary, but comes with a A$175 price tag.

Longrain

85 Commonwealth Street, Surry Hills; tel: 9280 2888; www.longrain.com.au; Mon–Thu 6pm–late, Fri noon–late, Sat–Sun 5.30pm–late; $$$

Sydney's glam crowd flocks to this converted 100-year-old warehouse both for its chic bar with some of the best cocktails in town, and for the adjoining restaurant that turns Thai food into high art. Do not let the communal tables fool you: prices are far from cheap, but dishes such as grilled veal ribs with coconut sauce and hot sour salad are worth it.

Mohr Fish

202 Devonshire Street, Surry Hills; www.mohrfish.com.au; tel: 9318 1326; Mon–Thu 11.30am–3:00pm & 5pm–10pm, Fri–Sun 11am–10pm; $–$$

This tiny, unpretentious fish and chippery is nearly 25 years old. It doesn't take bookings and most patrons end up nursing a beer in the pub next door while waiting for a table to clear. The wait is worth it. The menu sticks to simple fish dishes, but the fish selection is

Sean's Panaroma

fantastic and beautifully cooked, while entrees range from fish dumplings to mussel bouillabaisse.

Nepalese Kitchen

481 Crown Street, Surry Hills; tel: 9319 4264; daily until late; $

A tiny little unpretentious place that's become a favourite with locals - this restaurant serves delicious Nepalese fare in an informal setting. For the best experience, go with a group and order several dishes to share.

Una's

338–40 Victoria Street, Darlinghurst; tel: 9360 6885; www.unas.com.au; daily noon–late; $

The hip Victoria Street strip is perhaps the last place you would expect to find an old-fashioned Austrian diner, but Una's has held onto its prime position for more than three decades, making it older than many of its clientele. Una's is famous for serving up huge portions of hearty fare, whether it's a laden breakfast platter or a plate of veal schnitzel that still gets you change from a twenty.

Bondi

Barzura

62 Carr Street, Coogee, tel: 02 9665-5546, www.barzura.com.au; daily 7am-late; $$

Watch the sun rise over the Pacific and return for lunch, dinner or a late-night drink at this chilled out beachside venue. The menu boasts modern Aus-

tralian cooking, with influences ranging from Greek to Cajun, and the rockstar view across Coogee Beach adds extra sizzle.

North Bondi Italian

118–20 Ramsgate Avenue, North Bondi; tel: 9300 4400; www.idrb.com; Mon–Fri 5pm-late, Sat–Sun midday–late; $$–$$$

In some ways, this restaurant is quintessential Bondi. It has the beachside location and the hip factor, evident in everything from the chic dining room and the good-looking staff to the throng of gorgeous young things who seem to be perpetually waiting for a table (there's a no-bookings policy). What may come as a surprise, however, is the menu, which skips the pizza and pastas for truly inspired Italian cuisine.

Pompei's

126–30 Roscoe Street, Bondi Beach; tel: 9365 1233; www.pompeis.com.au; Fri–Sun noon–late, Tue–Thu 5pm–late; $–$$

If you are desperate for dinner at 6pm, you may need to find somewhere else as it is rush hour at this family-friendly joint, with children and prams tucked into every cranny. At other times though, Pompei's offers quality Italian a block from the beach. Thin-crust pizza, homemade pasta and fruity sorbets are deserved favourites.

Sean's Panaroma

270 Campbell Parade, Bondi Beach; tel: 02

Doyle's on the Beach

9365 4924; www.seanspanaroma.com.au; Wed–Fri 6pm–late, Saturday noon–late, Sun noon–2.30pm; $$$

Sean Moran likes to do things his way. His opening hours prove that, unlike most chefs, he appreciates having a life, another reason, perhaps, why he has stayed in the same location for years. Although his food could easily grace some of the city's most acclaimed dining rooms, he has stuck with this cosy beachside canteen, and his clientele love him for it.

Watsons Bay

Doyle's on the Beach

11 Marine Parade; tel: 9337 2007; www.doyles.com.au; Mon–Thu noon–3pm, Fri noon–3pm & 5.30pm–9pm, Sat–Sun noon–4pm & 5.30pm–9pm; $$$–$$$$

A chance to enjoy a million-dollar view is offered at the popular spot, and there are prices to match. The emphasis is on seafood, which is prepared simply and presented beautifully to the beachside tables.

Eastern Bay Thai

Unit 1, 3 Military Road, Watsons Bay; www.easternbay-thai.com.au; daily 5pm–9.30pm; $

Too far from the ferries to get silly-packed, this lovely little place serves authentic and unpretentious Thai tucker, including an excellent Hor-Mok Talay (an exotic seafood curry dish) and Phla Goong, a slightly spicier recipe with killer king prawns.

Manly

4 Pines Brewing Company

29/43-45 East Esplanade, Manly; tel: 9976 2300; www.4pinesbeer.com.au; daily 11am–midnight; $$

A crafty brewing den with a heady hipster menu and staff to match. Besides the yeasty feast, there's great food on tap here, delivered amid a sometimes raucous atmosphere and chased down with a selection of beautiful small-batch beers. Try the mouth-watering seafood bouillabaisse (featuring fresh crab, prawns, scallops, mussels and fish, with melted gruyere on housemade stout bread) or go for the classic roast, served during the famous Sunday session with a side order of live music.

Mobile

Eat Art Truck

Streets of Sydney; tel: 0410 665 178; www.eatarttruck.com; $

This restaurant comes to you – if you're lucky. If not, you'll have to chase it down – see the website for details on where Eat Art Truck is at any given time, or just follow the queue, who will be waiting for quality takeaway fare including slow-roasted beef brisket buns, nachos and pulled pork rolls. Service is swift, but during your short wait you can peruse the artwork on the side of the van, which is a space dedicated to emerging street artists, where a new painting is displayed each month.

Performance at the Belvoir Street Theatre

NIGHTLIFE

There's no defined arts precinct in Sydney, although the Sydney Theatre Company's two theatres have turned Walsh Bay into a fledgling hub. From converted stables in Kings Cross to reconfigured carriage halls in the inner west, venues are scattered across the city. This is by no means an exhaustive list, but does include the major venues for each art form.

Theatre

Belvoir Street Theatre

25 Belvoir Street, Surry Hills; tel: 9699 3444; www.belvoir.com.au

Geoffrey Rush and Cate Blanchett are just two of the actors who made their names with Company B, the talented troupe assembled by Neil Armfield, one of Australian theatre's great talents. The repertoire ranges from classic to new international hits, and fresh local talent. The Upstairs Theatre seats 350, while the intimate 80-seater Downstairs space hosts fringe productions.

The Stables

10 Nimrod Street, Kings Cross; tel: 9332 1052; www.griffintheatre. com.au

This tiny theatre, located in a former stables in the backstreets of Kings Cross, is home to the Griffin Theatre Company, which has a reputation for discovering and breaking in fresh young talent. Mondays are pay-what-you-can nights (minimum A$10).

The Wharf

Pier 4 and 5 Hickson Road, Walsh Bay; tel: 9250 1777; www.sydneytheatre. com.au

The Sydney Theatre Company (STC) boasts a stunning home in an atmospheric converted wharf. The STC's typically crowd-pleasing roster has got a bit adventurous of late, with international performers such as Liv Ullman popping in to direct. Their second venue, previously known as Sydney Theatre but recently renamed the Roslyn Packer Theatre (22 Hickson Road, Walsh Bay; tel: 9250 1999; www.roslynpacker theatre.com.au), is across the road from The Wharf.

Dance

Carriageworks

245 Wilson Street, Eveleigh; tel: 8571 9099; www.carriageworks.com.au

This beautifully converted train repair yard is one of Sydney's newest venues. It hosts performances from the Sydney Dance Company, the indigenous Bangarra Dance Theatre, and visiting troupes. Fans of industrial architecture will love its interior, while the performers love the expansive, adaptable stage.

Dancers at the Sydney Opera House

Classical music

City Recital Hall

Angel Place; tel: 8256 2222;
www.cityrecitalhall.com

This low-key venue in the heart of the CBD regularly hosts performances from Australia's most acclaimed classical ensembles, including the Brandenburg Orchestra. Particularly worth catching are performances by the Australian Chamber Orchestra, known for its varied programme of classics and new commissions, and for the A$10 million Del Gesù antique violin, rumoured to have once belonged to Paganini, played by orchestra leader, Richard Tognetti.

Sydney Opera House

Bennelong Point; tel: 9250 7777;
www.sydneyoperahouse.com

Do not let the name fool you; there is much more than classical music on offer at the Opera House. It is home to several of Australia's flagship performing arts companies, including Opera Australia and the Sydney Symphony Orchestra, and is the Sydney venue for the Melbourne-based Australian Ballet. In addition, the Drama Theatre and the Playhouse focus on mainstream theatre, including productions by Bell Shakespeare, Australia's only theatre company dedicated to the Bard. The intimate Studio offers a range of cutting-edge local and overseas dramatic and musical productions.

Jazz

The Basement

7 Macquarie Place, Circular Quay; tel: 9251 2797; www.thebasement.com.au

For decades Sydney's premier jazz and blues venue, The Basement has hosted all the big names, including Dizzy Gillespie, Herbie Hancock and Prince. World music, pop and alternative acts also make appearances at this wonderfully intimate venue. Early birds can book a table for dinner, guaranteeing you the best seats in the house.

Venue 505

280 Cleveland Street, Surry Hills;
http://venue505.com

With regular jazz on Monday nights, this is an artist-run performance space that features a range of live music and original performance art across several genres.

Woollahra Hotel

116 Queen Street, Woollahra; tel: 9327 9777; www.woollahrahotel.com.au

This sleek eastern-suburbs watering hole has live jazz on Sunday nights, and Sydney's best world music on Thursday nights, with everything from Brazilian funk to Afro-Cuban jazz. Once you have worked up an appetite on the dance floor, enjoy a Wagyu beefburger upstairs in the Moncur Terrace bistro.

Contemporary music

Enmore Theatre

118–132 Enmore Road, Newtown; tel:

9550 3666; www.enmoretheatre.com.au
Generations of Sydneysiders have watched their favourite bands grind it out on the stage of the Art Deco Enmore Theatre, Sydney's oldest running live music venue. From international headliners to local faves, they all play here. The building's faded glory is part of its charm, and the acoustics are excellent.

Goodgod Small Club

55 Liverpool St Chinatown; tel: 8084 0587; www.goodgodgoodgod.com
A small venue with a big heart and plenty of attitude, this place bounces to an alternative beat with live performances across lots of genres.

Metro Theatre

624 George Street; tel: 9550 3666; www.metrotheatre.com.au
A good old-fashioned rock venue in the heart of the CBD, with a pumping mosh pit and sticky floors. Lots of international bands play here, notably rock and hip-hop acts. Its central location makes it easy to catch a taxi home.

Oxford Art Factory

38–46 Oxford Street, Darlinghurst; tel: 9332 3711; www.oxfordartfactory.com
Recently, the Oxford Art Factory has established itself as a hub for all kinds of art. In addition to the exhibitions on the walls, the Live Art Space hosts international and local performers from genres ranging from rock and pop to burlesques and cabaret. The bar is a cool place to chill out.

Film

Dendy Opera Quays

Shop 9, 2 East Circular Quay; tel: 9247 3800; www.dendy.com.au
Dendy Films is Australia's premier arthouse chain, and this is the jewel in their crown, perched on the edge of Sydney's foreshore. The best of local and foreign arthouse films are screened here and you can enjoy a glass of wine with your film.

The Verona

17 Oxford Street, Paddington; tel: 9360 6099; www.palacecinemas.com.au
Another favourite with the arthouse crowd, The Verona wins points for its Oxford Street location, which makes it easy to grab a bite after the show. Its major drawback is the box office on the pavement, which makes queuing for popular sessions a drag. Get your tickets early, then browse through the excellent Ariel bookshop opposite.

Bars and clubs

Arthouse Hotel

275 Pitt Street; tel: 9284 1200; www.thearthousehotel.com.au
This is a centrally located venue in a heritage building that has something for everyone. Urban sophisticates head upstairs for the stunning 19th-century architecture, the sleek design and the refined vibe. Huge raves downstairs

Band at the Enmore Theatre

on Friday and Saturday nights attract a younger crowd. There's a decent restaurant too.

Blu Bar on 36

Shangri-La Hotel, 176 Cumberland Street; tel: 9250 6013; www.shangri-la.com/sydney
Not content with offering possibly the best view in Sydney, Blu Horizon also has a great cocktail list. Take the express lift to the top, where you will be dazzled by the stellar harbour view from floor-to-ceiling windows.

The Ivy Bar

330 George Street; tel: 9240 3000; www.merivale.com.au
Justin Hemmes is Sydney's king of cool, the man behind some of the city's best-loved pleasure palaces, including Establishment and Slip Inn, where a Danish crown prince met his Australian princess. The Ivy (which includes 18 bars, nine restaurants and 11 shops) is just one of his ventures, and its centrepiece is The Ivy Bar, a sleek space where you can pose at the bar, curl up in a corner, or simply dance the night away…as long as you are cool enough to get past the door staff.

Shady Pines Saloon

256 Crown Street, Darlinghurst; http://shadypinessaloon.com
In a small lane behind Oxford Street, you'll find a Sydney barfly institution (if you can get past the queue). Shady Pines Saloon is a unique place, where stuffed animals look across a dimly lit bar with a killer cocktail list.

Gay and lesbian venues

Oxford Street is the epicentre of gay Sydney, with a range of venues catering for all tastes. Hotspots include the super-sleek Slide (41 Oxford Street, Darlinghurst; tel: 8915 1899; www.slide.com.au; Wed–Sun until late), housed in a former bank and offering a dining and cabaret show as well as a buzzing dance floor. Old favourites include the welcoming Colombian Hotel (corner Oxford and Crown streets, Darlinghurst; tel: 9360 2151; www.colombian.com.au; Mon–Fri 9am–6am, Sat–Sun 11am–6am) and Midnight Shift (85 Oxford Street, Darlinghurst; tel: 9360 4319; www.themidnightshift.com; daily until late): the drag shows upstairs are well worth the price of admission, while there's no cover charge at the downstairs bar.

If your idea of a good time is dancing the night away, try the pumping Arq (16 Flinders Street, Taylor Square; tel: 9380 8700; www.arqsydney.com.au; Fri 11pm–Mon 6am). Away from Oxford Street, venues include Newtown's Bank Hotel (324 King Street; tel: 02 8568 1900; www.bankhotel.com.au; open daily until late), where punters have the choice between moody interiors or a multi-level beer garden. Wednesdays are for ladies; another popular lesbian venue nearby is The Sly Fox (199 Enmore Road, Enmore; tel: 9557 1016; Wed–Sun; 10am–late).

Kangaroos, Aussie icons

A–Z

A

Age restrictions

The age of consent for both heterosexual and homosexual sex in New South Wales is 16.

Drivers must be aged 18 to obtain a licence.

To drink or buy alcohol, or smoke any tobacco product, people must be at least 18 years old.

B

Budgeting

Average costs (in Australian dollars) for a range of items are listed below:

beer/glass of house wine: A$6
main course at a budget restaurant: A$20
main course at a moderate restaurant: A$30
main course at an expensive restaurant: A$50
cheap hotel: A$150
moderate hotel: A$250
deluxe hotel: A$350
taxi to the airport: A$35
single bus ticket: A$3.80 (3–5 sections)
TravelTen (10 bus rides): A$30.40 (3–5 sections)
My Multi Day Pass (can be used on bus, train and ferry): A$24

C

Children

Sydney is a great destination for families and children, with lots of parklands and beaches offering play opportunities, as well as exciting attractions. Children travel at reduced prices on public transport and pay reduced admission at most attractions. Most hotels offer babysitting services. At many hotels and child-friendly attractions, you will find a copy of *Sydney's Child*, a free monthly magazine with handy information and offers.

Clothing

Sydney is an informal and relaxed city with a temperate climate, which takes a lot of the stress out of packing. Concentrate on lightweight clothing that can be worn in layers if you are travelling in warmer months. Even in winter, you will not need heavy woollies – a 12°C (54°F) day is considered by Sydneysiders to be very cold. Casual clothes are acceptable in most places, and barely anyone will bat an eyelid if you reveal some flesh. Just bear in mind that Sydneysiders are body-obsessed: those who have great bodies can and do show them off.

Consulates

British Consulate General, Level 16, 1 Macquarie Place; tel: 02 9247 7521;

Giraffe at Taronga Zoo – lots of animals, indigenous and otherwise, to appeal to children

www.ukinaustralia.fco.gov.uk.

Consulate General of Canada, Level 5, 111 Harrington Street; tel: 02 9364 3000; www.canadainternational.gc.ca.

Consulate General of Ireland, Level 26, 1 Market Street; tel: 02 9264 9635; www.irishconsulatesydney.net.

Consulate General of the USA, MLC Centre, Level 59, 19–29 Martin Place; tel: 02 9373 9200; http://sydney.usconsulate.gov.

Crime and safety

Common-sense rules apply when visiting Sydney. As in any popular tourist destination, petty theft can be an issue at popular sights. Keep wallets out of sight and don't leave valuables visible in the car or luggage unattended.

The inner-city is, on the whole, quite safe. Despite its slightly unsavoury reputation, visitors to Kings Cross are unlikely to encounter trouble – unless they are looking for it – thanks to the constant urban buzz and a regular police presence. It is best to avoid Hyde Park after 10pm, though, particularly if you are on your own.

During off-peak periods, many city and suburban railway stations are either unstaffed or equipped with a skeleton staff. Look for 'night safe' areas on the platforms, which have security cameras and an intercom for contacting staff.

On a train, a blue light on one of the carriages indicates a guard is travelling in the carriage. Generally, public transport in the inner city is safe at any time of day. Avoid longer trips after 10pm, when there are fewer passengers.

Customs

Australia has extremely strict quarantine laws, to protect the agricultural industries and native Australian flora and fauna from introduced diseases. Animals, plants and their derivatives (feathers, untreated wood, fur, etc) must be declared on arrival, along with all foodstuffs, no matter how well packaged (and even if you've been given them on the plane – it can work out to be a very expensive apple if you try and take it with you…). All passengers must fill in an Incoming Passenger Card before disembarking the plane, which is checked by customs officers. There are serious penalties for false declarations. In many cases, you will be allowed to keep the items, as long as you declare them.

Anyone over the age of 18 is allowed to bring into Australia: A\$900 worth of goods (A\$450 for those under 18), not including alcohol or tobacco; 2.25l of alcohol (wine, beer or spirits); and 250 cigarettes or 250g of cigars and tobacco products other than cigarettes.

Disabled travellers

Sydney caters reasonably well for people with disabilities, but it is wise to start making enquiries and arrangements before leaving home. A good

place to begin is the *National Information Communication Awareness Network (NICAN)*, a national organisation that keeps a database of facilities and services with disabled access, including accommodation and tourist sights. It also keeps track of the range of publications on the subject.

IDEAS (Information on Disability Awareness and Education Services) also offers online databases on disability services, equipment suppliers and accessible travel, plus other speciality information from other agencies.

Most larger hotels – apart from the more moderately priced ones – have lifts. Metro Monorail and LightRail services are wheelchair-accessible, as are some buses (indicated on timetables available at bus stops or online at www.sydneybuses.info).

For more information, see *NICAN*, tel: 1800 806 769; www.nican.com.au and *IDEAS*, tel: 1800 029 904; www.ideas.org.au.

E

Electricity

The Australian power supply is 220–240 volts AC. Sockets are three flat-pin plugs and electrical items from the US and Europe, including the UK, will require an adaptor plug.

Emergencies

For police, fire or ambulance, call 000. From a mobile phone, try calling 112 if you are having trouble getting reception or signal (this is a secondary emergency number, available from all GSM or GSM derived mobile phones, which works all over the world and will automatically default to the national emergency service closest to you) – or 106, which connects to the text-based relay service for people who have a hearing or speech impairment.

Hotel Doctor Service: tel: 02 9962 6000

Dental Emergency Information Service: tel: 02 9369 7050

Etiquette

Australians take a casual approach to matters of etiquette. If you are greeting someone, saying 'G'day' will instantly mark you out as a tourist; 'Hello' and 'Hi' are much more commonly used. Australians are far less likely than Europeans to open doors for women, although it is not unheard of. The one rule of etiquette no Australian will break: if someone 'shouts' you (buys you a drink), the next round is your turn. Similarly, it is considered bad form not to bring along some kind of alcoholic beverage if you are invited to someone's house for dinner.

F

Festivals and holidays

Sydney's favourite festivals are grand spectaculars, whether they involve the drag and dazzle of the Gay and Les-

The Sydney skyline by night

bian Mardi Gras or the spectacular harbour firework celebrations on New Year's Eve. Possibly Australia's most important national holiday, Anzac Day, commemorates the first major military action fought by Australian and New Zealand forces during World War I when they landed at Gallipolli on 25 April 1915, suffering huge losses (over 8,000 Australian soldiers died in the eight-month long Allied offensive). Read below for information on some of the city's best festivals, and for further information on events in Sydney check www.sydneyfestivals.com.au and www.cityofsydney.nsw.gov.au:

January
Sydney Festival: Three weeks of local and international arts.
Australia Day (26 Jan): Various harbour-centred events, including the inevitable fireworks.

February
Chinese New Year: Lion dances, parades, markets and other festivities centred around Chinatown.

February/March
Gay and Lesbian Mardi Gras: a parade, party and associated arts festival.

Easter
Royal Easter Show: The country comes to town; from wood-chopping to cattle contests.

May
Sydney Writers Festival: A varied programme of readings, public lectures and panel events, many of which are free.

June
Sydney Film Festival: Two weeks of local and international cinema, centred around the gorgeous State Theatre.

September
Spring Racing Carnival: Sydney's premier horse racing event is the place to be seen.

December
Sydney to Hobart Yacht Race: Thousands flock to the foreshore to watch the start of the race.

New Year's Eve
The biggest party of them all; if you want to nab a foreshore position for the best view of the fireworks, be prepared to camp out all day.

Further reading

For more information, see page 136.

Aboriginal Australia
The Hard Light of Day, Rod Moss
Archaeology of the Dreaming, Josephine Flood.
Dreamings: The Art of Aboriginal Australia, edited by Peter Sutton.
The Whispering in Our Hearts, Henry Reynolds.

Gay ~ Lesbian

Proud

Sydney has a thriving gay scene

Art and architecture
The Art of Australia, Robert Hughes.
Sydney: A Guide to Recent Architecture, Francesca Morrison.
Sydney Architecture, Graham Jahn.

Biography
A Fence Around the Cuckoo, Ruth Park.
30 Days in Sydney, Peter Carey.
Unreliable Memoirs, Clive James.

Fiction
The Secret River, Kate Grenville
King of the Cross, Mark Dapin
He Died with a Felafel in His Hand, John Birmingham
For Love Alone, Christina Stead.
A Harp in the South, Ruth Park.
Oscar and Lucinda, Peter Carey.
Poor Man's Orange, Ruth Park.
The Service of Clouds, Delia Falconer.

Food and wine
The Penguin Good Australian Wine Guide, Mark Shield and Huon Hooke.
The SBS Eating Guide, Maeve O'Mara and Joanna Savill.
The Sydney Morning Herald Good Food Guide, edited by Terry Durack and Jill Dupleix.
The Wines of Australia, Oliver Mayo.

History
The Fatal Shore, Robert Hughes.
The Future Eaters, Tim Flannery.
Leviathan, John Birmingham.
A Secret Country, John Pilger.

Travel Companions
Best Sydney Bushwalks, Neil Paton.
A Companion Guide to Sydney, Ruth Park.
Cosmopolitan Sydney: Explore the World in One City, Jock Collins and Antonio Castillo.
Sydney, Jan Morris.
The Sydney Morning Herald Best of Sydney, edited by Ross Muller.
Good bookstores in Sydney include:
Dymocks (424 George Street; www.dymocks.com.au)
Kinokunyia (500 George Street; www.kinokuniya.com)
Borders Bondi Junction (500 Oxford Street; www.borders.com.au)

Gay and lesbian travellers

Sydney is one of the world's queer capitals, where homosexuality is not only legal (the age of consent is 16), but homosexuals are legally protected against discrimination and defamation (although the conservative government has dug its heels in and rejected the idea of a referendum on gay marriage thus far, but a movement is growing). That does not mean there is no homophobia, of course, but the inner city – particularly the gay hotspots of Darlinghurst and Newtown – is particularly gay-friendly, as you will see most spectacularly during the annual Mardi Gras.

Held each February, Mardi Gras is

Soaking up the sun on Bondi Beach

a three-week-long party, ending in a parade and huge ticket-only all-night dance party. Useful resources before your visit include sites such as www.pridecentre.com.au, www.pinkboard.com.au and www.dreadedned.com.au, where you will find information on bars, clubs, restaurants, hotels, saunas and shops. Once you arrive, pick up a copy of the two free weekly gay mags, *Sydney Star Observer* and *Q Magazine*, for up-to-date information.

Green issues

Australia has the unhappy distinction of having one of the most fragile environments on earth, as well as one of the world's largest per capita ecological footprints, which makes climate change a major issue for the country. After years of neglect by the Coalition government of Prime Minster John Howard, environmental issues were being addressed by the Labor government that came into power in 2007. However, the Coalition were elected back into office in 2013, and the then Prime Minister, Tony Abbott, publically said he believed the argument behind climate change to be 'absolute crap', so backwards steps were taken, including the repeal of the Carbon Tax. Time will tell if his recent successor, Malcolm Turnbull, takes a different line.

On a day-to-day level, however, Australians are quite environmentally aware, dutifully recycling paper, plastics and glass, and being very anti-littering.

The city's biggest environmental events are both held in March. Clean Up Australia Day sounds exactly like what it is, while Earth Hour, a now-global initiative that launched in Sydney in 2007, turns the city's lights off for an hour to demonstrate a commitment to combating climate change.

Air travel produces a huge amount of carbon dioxide and is a major contributor to global warming. If you would like to offset the damage caused to the environment by your flight, a number of organisations can do this for you, using online 'carbon calculators', which tell you how much you need to donate. In the UK travellers can visit www.climatecare.org or www.carbonneutral.com; in the US log on to www.climatefriendly.com or www.sustainabletravelinternational.org.

Health

Healthcare and insurance

The UK and Ireland have reciprocal healthcare agreements with Australia that entitle visitors to free hospital treatment through the Medicare system. This does not cover all eventualities, however; ambulance and dental treatment, for instance, are not included. All travellers should take out their own travel insurance, and check the fine print to see whether you need to register with Medicare before making a claim.

Inoculations

No vaccinations are required for entry to Australia, unless you have been in an epidemic zone or a yellow fever-, cholera- or typhoid-infested area in the six days prior to your arrival.

Pharmacies and hospitals

Chemists (pharmacies) are a great place to get advice on minor ailments such as bites, scratches and stomach trouble. They will also tell you where the nearest medical centre is. If you have a prescription from your doctor that you want to get filled in Australia, you will need to have it endorsed by a local medical practitioner. While most public hospitals have emergency departments, these are notoriously overstretched. For anything that is not a major condition, you are advised to find the nearest medical centre instead.

The **Crest Hotel Pharmacy** (91–93 Darlinghurst Road; tel: 9358 1822) in Kings Cross is open from 8am to midnight, seven days a week.

Hours and holidays

Business hours are generally 9am to 5pm Monday to Friday. Shops will generally stay open to 6pm on weekdays and 9pm on Thursdays, with weekend opening hours usually 10am to 5pm on Saturdays and 10am to 4pm on Sundays. Banks, post offices and most shops close on the following public holidays:

1 Jan New Year's Day.
26 Jan Australia Day.
Mar/Apr Good Friday, Easter Monday.
25 Apr Anzac Day.
June (2nd Mon) Queen's Birthday.
Aug (1st Mon) Bank Holiday.
Oct (1st Mon) Labour Day.
25 Dec Christmas Day.
26 Dec Boxing Day.

I

Internet facilities

Many Sydney cafes offer Wi-Fi access to paying patrons armed with their own device (phone, tablet or laptop), and in common with other cities, Internet cafes are increasingly rare. A few exist still around the backpacker hub of Kings Cross. Try **Global Gossip** (63 Darlinghurst Road, Kings Cross; www.globalgossip.com), with branches around the city.

L

Left luggage

Sydney's stations do not provide left-luggage facilities. For storage lockers in the CBD, try CBD Storage at World Square (http://www.cbdstorage.com.au/0lugg age.aspx).

Lost property

There are separate lost-property offices at each Sydney bus depot. To contact the appropriate depot, visit www.sydney buses.info/lost-property.

The city's enticing blend of old and new architecture

CityRail's lost-property office is located at Central Station, opposite platform 1, and is open from 8.30am to 4.20pm Monday to Friday. Call 9379 3341, or fill in an online request at www.sydneytrains.info/contact_us/lost_property if you need to report a loss.

M

Maps

You can pick up regional maps at the Sydney Visitor Centre (corner of Argyle and Playfair streets, The Rocks; tel: 9255 1788; www.shfa.nsw.gov.au; daily 9.30am–5.30pm). You can download bus maps from www.sydneybuses.info; newsagents usually also carry maps for local bus routes.

Media

Print media

Sydney has just one broadsheet newspaper, *The Sydney Morning Herald*, and one tabloid, *The Daily Telegraph*. There are now two excellent online papers, though, the Australian *Guardian* (www.theguardian.com/au) and *The Conversation* (http://theconversation.com). The national broadsheet, *The Australian*, and the national business newspaper, *The Australian Financial Review*, are also widely available. A weekly entertainment guide comes free with Friday's *Herald*, and many free visitor-oriented publications are available at hotels and other tourist destinations. The monthly *Time Out* and free street press such as *Drum Media* are available in pubs and record shops.

Radio

Sydney has a broad range of radio stations to choose from, with popular FM stations including ABC Classic FM (92.9) for classical; MIX 106.5FM for music that falls between rock and pop; and the ABC's youth station, Triple J (105.9), for alternative music.

Television

Australia's five free-to-air channels have been instrumental in rolling out digital television, with 15 digital stations now available, and more to come. The national broadcaster, the ABC, has the best national news and current affairs coverage; the other government-run station, the more internationally oriented SBS, features dramas, documentaries and movies from around the world, as well as international news.

The commercial channels, Seven, Nine and Ten, are fairly interchangeable, although Ten caters to a younger audience than the other two. Satellite television is also available in most hotels.

Money

Cash machines

There are hundreds of Automatic Teller Machines (ATMs) around the city, allowing for easy withdrawal of cash.

Credit cards

American Express, Visa and Master-Card are all readily accepted, with Diners Club less popular. Some restaurants and companies levy a credit-card charge, usually around 1 or 2 percent.

Currency

The local currency is the Australian dollar (abbreviated as A$ or simply $), made up of 100 cents. Coins come in 5-, 10-, 20- and 50-cent units, and A$1 and A$2 units. Notes come in A$5, A$10, A$20, A$50 and A$100 denominations. Where prices feature single cents, these are rounded up or down to the nearest 5 cents.

Taxes

A Goods and Services Tax (GST) of 10 percent is levied virtually across the board (there are a few exemptions). By law, the GST must be included in the advertised price of an item.

Tipping

Australians are generally fairly relaxed about tipping. While it has become common to leave 10 percent at a restaurant, it is not customary to tip taxi drivers, hairdressers, bar staff or porters at airports.

Travellers' cheques

All well-known Australian-dollar travellers' cheques can be cashed at airports, banks, hotels and similar establishments. Banks offer the best exchange rates on cheques in foreign currencies; most banks charge a fee for cashing cheques.

Police

In an emergency, dial 000; for non-emergency enquiries, telephone police assistance on 131 444.

Post

The government-run Australia Post delivers an efficient, if expensive, service. Buy your stamps and post your letters at any post office (expect to pay A$1.45 to send a postcard to Europe or the US, and A$2.20 for a standard letter). There are plenty of red post boxes on the streets that you can also use. Yellow post boxes are for the Overnight Express service, which delivers to most places in Australia and costs extra. (To use this service, you need to buy a special envelope at the post office.) The General Post Office (GPO) is located in Martin Place, on the corner of George Street, www.austpost.com.au.

You can buy stamps at all post offices and at some newsagents. For assured next-day delivery within Australia it is possible to buy special Express Post envelopes. Otherwise, mail takes between one and three days to be delivered. The cost of overseas mail depends on the weight and size of the item. Standard overseas mail takes about a week to most destinations.

A rare spot of rain

R

Religion

The Australian Constitution specifically prohibits the establishment of a state religion, but according to the latest census, around two-thirds of Australians still identify themselves as Christians. The next most popular religions are Buddhism and Islam. As in many other Western countries, the integration of Islamic communities has become an issue that flares up periodically – notably after the hostage situation in Martin Place in late 2014. On the whole, however, Australia remains a tolerant, diverse nation.

S

Smoking

Australia has world-leading and very strong anti-smoking legislation that bans smoking inside offices, shopping centres, restaurants, public buildings, licensed premises, public transport and even on some beaches. Cigarette packets are not now allowed to feature a logo or any marketing, and instead revel horrific images of smoking-caused diseases.

T

Telephones

To call Sydney from outside the country, dial your international access code followed by 61 for Australia and 2 for Sydney. To call anywhere else in Australia from Sydney, dial the area code (eg 03 for Melbourne, 07 for Brisbane), followed by the number. You do not need to dial 02 to call a Sydney number when in Sydney, nor do you add 02 to six-digit numbers beginning with 13.

To call internationally from Sydney, dial 0011 followed by the relevant country code (Canada 1, Ireland 353, UK 44, US 1).

Public phone boxes are hard to find and their design means they are noisy to use if you do; your best bet is a station or major post office.

Mobile (cell) phones

Australia uses the 900MHz and 1,800MHz GSM bands for mobile phones. Many North American phones, which are CDMA-band only, will not work in Australia. If you want to buy a local SIM card, you can purchase one at the many mobile-phone shops throughout the city. Expect to pay around A$20–30. A phone and SIM card pack, with a basic phone and around A$10 in phone credit, can start as low as around A$60.

Before buying a phone or SIM card, check which areas are covered, as different service providers offer different levels of coverage (although all will work in the main cities). Note that in Australia, the person calling the mobile phone pays; receiving a call on a mobile is free.

See the city from above for stunning views

Time zones

Sydney is on Eastern Standard Time (along with the rest of New South Wales, Queensland, Victoria and Tasmania). This is GMT +10. At noon in Sydney, it is 2am in London, and 9pm the day before in New York.

During the summer, New South Wales observes Daylight Saving Time, moving the clock forward by one hour between the first Sunday in October and the last Sunday in March. At noon in Sydney, it is therefore 1am in London and 8pm the day before in New York.

Toilets

Pay-to-use public toilets are fairly common on Sydney streets, but you can generally use the facilities at any pub or department store free of charge without making a purchase. Toilets are generally well maintained.

Tourist information

The Sydney Visitor Centre (corner of Argyle and Playfair streets, The Rocks; tel: 02 9255 1788; www.shfa.nsw.gov.au; daily 9.30am–5.30pm) is a useful resource for travellers, with plenty of printed material and knowledgeable staff. The website also has some helpful features to access before your trip, including the ability to book accommodation for you.

Tours and guides

A harbour cruise remains a must-do for many visitors, although you can get a very similar experience at a much cheaper price simply by catching a ferry to a destination such as Taronga Zoo or Manly. A number of operators offer a wide range of similar cruises: among the most experienced is Captain Cook Cruises (www.captaincook.com.au/sydney). Other options include include sailing on an authentic timber tall ship, courtesy of Sydney Tall Ships (www.sydneytallships.com.au), or the unique Tribal Warrior cruise, which offers an indigenous perspective (www.tribalwarrior.org).

Transport

Arrival

By air

International airlines land at Sydney's international airport, Kingsford Smith Airport at Mascot, approximately 8km (5 miles) from the city centre. AirportLink trains (www.airportlink.com.au) run to and from Central Station up to eight times an hour on weekdays, and four times an hour at weekends; the journey takes 12 minutes, and a single adult journey costs around A$15.

Many hotels run shuttle buses to the airport. A taxi to the city centre will cost about A$30 and take about 20 minutes in light traffic. Each terminal has its own taxi rank.

If you intend to hire a car, all the major companies have offices at the airport terminals.

By sea

If time and money permit, there is no better introduction to this harbour city

A giant cruise liner in port

than arriving by boat. Ocean liners berth at the Overseas Passenger Terminal in Circular Quay and at Barangaroo.

Getting around
Tickets and passes

Most locals use Opal cards (www.opal.com.au), which cover travel on all Sydney's public transport, including trains, ferries, buses and light rail, or TravelTen bus tickets (colour-coded depending on which areas you want to travel in). These are both good options because a growing number of buses are prepay only, so you need already to have purchased your ticket; they also offer (small) savings. There are combined monorail/light rail one- and three-day passes, but these do not work with any other form of transport. If you are staying for a week and travelling every day, consider using a MyMulti, which can be used on buses, trains and ferries. This can be good value if you are going to be doing a lot of travelling. You can also get a MyMulti DayPass, a one-day ticket for bus, train and ferry, but you would need to be covering a huge amount of territory to make this worthwhile.

Buses

Sydney's extensive bus service has its main termini at Circular Quay, Wynyard and Central Station. Red Sydney Explorer and blue Bondi Explorer hop-on hop-off buses leave regularly from Circular Quay and run in a continuous loop around the city's main attractions. You can buy a one- or a two-day (valid for any two days out of eight) ticket. For timetables or routes call Transport Infoline; tel: 131 500; www.131500.com.au. A free CBD shuttle (route no. 555) operates every 10 minutes during peak hours (Mon–Fri 9.30am–3.30pm, Sat–Sun 9.30am–6pm).

Driving

Sydneysiders have a reputation for being aggressive drivers, which many blame on the hazards facing the city's motorists: congestion, frequent toll roads, the difficulty of finding parking anywhere in the city – and, if you do find it, the cost of parking meters – and speed limits that can change several times in the space of a few kilometres. However, drivers follow the road rules; so as long as you are comfortable driving on the left, you will be fine.

One thing to beware of is drink driving. There are heavy penalties for this; up to imprisonment for serious transgression. Random breath-testing is common. The limit for licensed drivers is 0.05g per 100ml.

Hiring a car in Australia is expensive by international standards. The main companies – Avis, Hertz and Budget – have nearidentical prices. Small outfits may offer cheaper rates, but won't provide the same coverage. Overseas drivers aged 18 or older only need to be in possession of an up-to-date driving licence from their home country. For information about road rules visit www.rta.nsw.gov.au/rulesregulations/roadrules.

Ferries

Sydney's most picturesque form of transport is loved by both commuters and tourists; most services begin and end at Circular Quay. Tickets and timetables can be found at the ferries office here, or at www.sydneyferries. info.

Metro Light Rail and Monorail

The Light Rail links the CBD with the inner-west suburbs, while the monorail is an elevated track around Darling Harbour, Chinatown and the CBD. The CBD and South East line is a future line that will operate from Circular Quay at the northern end of the Central Business District to Central station. For more information on either service, visit www. metrotransport.com.au.

Taxis

Taxis can be hailed in the street or at a taxi rank, and should run on a meter. There is an initial A\$3.20 charge, then A\$1.93 per km thereafter. This rises by 20 percent between 10pm and 6am. Booking a taxi by phone will incur surcharges, as will journeys on toll roads.

Companies include:

Premier Cabs, tel: 131 017.

Taxis Combined, tel: 133 300.

Legion Cabs, tel: 131 451.

For more information, visit www.nsw taxi.org.au.

Water taxis are a handy way for getting to waterfront attractions, but can be expensive unless several of you share the cost. Water Taxis Combined, tel: 02 9555 888; www.watertaxis.com.au.

Trains

Cityrail services provide fast links through Sydney's inner city and the suburbs, but tend to be very congested at peak hours. Trains run until midnight, when they are replaced by a Nightrider bus service. All suburban lines stop at Town Hall and Central Station, which is also Sydney's main terminal for regional and interstate trains.

V

Visas and passports

Visitors to Australia must have a passport valid for the entire period of their stay. Anyone who is not an Australian citizen also needs a visa, which must be obtained before leaving home, except for New Zealand citizens, who are issued with a visa on arrival in Australia.

Most visitors can obtain a visa online, using either the eVisitor service for European visitors (www.immi. gov.au/e_visa/evisitor.htm) or the Electronic Transfer Authority (www.eta. immi.gov.au) for visitors from other countries including the USA. Visas are generally valid for 12 months, with no stay exceeding three months. An online fee of around A\$20 applies. Tourist visas for longer than three months must be obtained from an embassy or consulate. Extending a visa depends on the visa type. ETAs and eVisitors cannot be extended; if you wanted to stay, you would need to apply for a different type of visa at

Taxi by night

least two weeks before your other visa expired.

Australia overseas

In the UK:

Australian High Commission, Australia House, The Strand, London WC2B 4LA; tel: 020-7379 4334; www.uk.embassy.gov.au.

In the US:

Australian Embassy, 1601 Massachusetts Avenue, NW Washington DC 20036; tel: 202-797 3000; www.usa.embassy.gov.au (plus consulates in New York, Los Angeles, San Francisco, Miami and Detroit).

In Canada:

Australian High Commission, Suite 710, 50 O'Connor Street, Ottawa, ON K1P 6L2; tel: 613-236 0841; http://canada.highcommission.gov.au/otwa/home.html.

W

Websites

Useful websites for sights and attractions are listed throughout the book. Try also www.sydneyguide.net.au, www.sydney.com.au, www.sydneyaustralia.com and www.eatability.com.au.

Women

Parts of Australia are still distinctly 'blokey', but Sydney is a modern metropolis with broadly progressive views on gender roles. The Lord Mayor of Sydney is a woman (Clover Moore, serving her third term) but Australia seemed to struggle with the concept of having a female prime minister – whatever you think of her politics, the treatment of Julia Gillard while she was in office by sections of the media was openly misogynistic.

Sydney is a fairly safe city for women travelling alone, but it's sensible to take normal precautions, especially when out at night.

Weights and measures

Australia uses the metric system of weights, measures and temperatures.

Bryan Brown and Heath Ledger in 'Two Hands'

BOOKS AND FILM

For all Melbourne's reputation as Australia's artistic heartland, Sydney has a proud literary and cinematic tradition, and the output and soaring success of the Harbour City's writers, filmmakers and actors speaks for itself.

Books

The city hosts the annual Sydney Writers' Festival (www.swf.org.au), the country's premier pen-jockey event, where the bill annually boasts critically acclaimed international authors as well as high-flying local raconteurs.

New South Wales produced two female authors whose names live on in the country's most coveted literary awards: Miles Franklin (1879–1954) a pioneering Australian writer and feminist best known for her novel *My Brilliant Career*, and Christina Stead (1902–1983) author of the highly personal *The Man Who Loved Children* and *For Love Alone*.

Sydney's most famous scribbling son was Patrick White, winner of the Nobel Prize in Literature in 1973. White's novels include *Voss*, which won the inaugural Miles Franklin Literary Award in 1957, a prize he won again with *Riders in the Chariot* (1961).

Sydney-born Geraldine Brooks won the Pulitzer Prize for Fiction for her 2005 novel, *March*. Her latest work, a historical novel set in the Dark Ages, *The Secret Chord*, was released in 2015.

Meanwhile, Sydneysider Kate Grenville won Britain's Orange Prize for Fiction with *The Idea of* Perfection in 2000, but caused even more of a stir with *The Secret River* (2006), a sublime but simultaneously searing novel about convict life in New South Wales and white–indigenous relationships in the early years of the colony. Inspired by the life story of her great, great, great grandfather, it was nominated for the Man Booker prize, and Grenville has since written two thematically connected books: *The Lieutenant* (2008), set before *Secret River*, and *Sarah Thornhill* (2011), set after it.

A far lighter account of life in the city and its surrounds can be enjoyed in the pages of Clive James' *Unreliable Memoirs*, where we meet the author and broadcaster coming of age in the suburbs of post-war Sydney.

For a biography of the city itself, go no further than the epic *Leviathan*, which saw British-born but Australia-raised author John Birmingham win Australia's National Prize For Non-Fiction in 2002.

Other novels that deal with the modern city include King of the Cross by Mark Dapin, a thinly fictionalised account of a local hood, which won the 2010 Ned Kelly Award (Australia's literary awards for crime writing).

The seedy side of Kings Cross is also the setting for *The Unknown Terrorist* by

Richard Flanagan, as he paints a picture of a paranoid Harbour City in the post 9/11 world. Flanagan – already highly respected for previous works *Death of a River Guide* (1994), *The Sound of One Hand Clapping* (1997) and *Gould's Book of Fish* (2001) – won the Man Booker prize in 2014 with *The Narrow Road to the Deep North*.

Film

The local film industry is strong too. Sydney is the home of the world's largest short film festival – Tropfest (www.tropfest.com). Going into its 23rd year, this now-iconic festival sees a shortlisted selection of mini films (made around a signature theme by a range of amateur and pro filmmakers) simultaneously screen at venues all around Australia, with a winner picked by a panel on the night.

It all began in the Tropicana Caffe in Sydney (see page 61), when a handful of shorts were shown to 200 people. Now the films are seen by around 150,000 people in Australia, and the idea has spread to New Zealand, South East Asia, the US and the Middle East. Tropfest has been described by Geoffrey Rush (Australian film royalty and one of the few people to ever win acting's triple crown: an Academy Award, a Tony Award and an Emmy Award) thus: "This is as close to rock and roll that filmmaking can ever get."

When it's not being used as a setting for film screenings, Sydney is often seen as the backdrop for some major productions. Nicole Kidman's career began here with *BMX Bandits* in 1983 and she has returned time and again, to shoot films such as Baz Luhrmann's epic *Australia* (2008).

Numerous high-profile projects have been filmed here, including *The Wolverine* (2013) starring one of Sydney's most famous sons, Hugh Jackson, and Star Wars episodes II *Attack of the Clones* (2002) and III *Revenge of the Sith* (2005), which both featured local lad Joel Edgerton.

The city itself – notably Kings Cross – played a big role in a fantastic film that launched the career of its lead man. *Two Hands* (1999) was Heath Ledger's first significant big screen role. Ledger seemed destined for greatness before his untimely death, winning critical accolades and awards for roles in *Brokeback Mountain* (2005), the Sydney-based *Candy* (2006), *The Dark Knight* (2008) and *The Imaginarium of Doctor Parnassus* (2009). The film also featured the talents of local legend Bryan Brown (*Cocktail, Dirty Deeds, Australia*) and Sydneysider Rose Byrne (*Damages, Troy, 28 Weeks Later, Bridesmaids*).

The latest batch of blockbusters to filmed in Sydney include *Pirates of the Caribbean 5: Dead Men Tell No Tales*, due for release in 2017, and starring young Aussie actor Brenton Thwaites alongside Johnny Depp and the master, Geoffrey Rush.

ABOUT THIS BOOK

This *Explore Guide* has been produced by the editors of Insight Guides, whose books have set the standard for visual travel guides since 1970. With top-quality photography and authoritative recommendations, these guidebooks bring you the very best routes and itineraries in the world's most exciting destinations.

BEST ROUTES

The routes in the book provide something to suit all budgets, tastes and trip lengths. As well as covering the destination's many classic attractions, the itineraries track lesser-known sights, and there are also excursions for those who want to extend their visit outside the city. The routes embrace a range of interests, so whether you are an art fan, a gourmet, a history buff or have kids to entertain, you will find an option to suit.

We recommend reading the whole of a route before setting out. This should help you to familiarise yourself with it and enable you to plan where to stop for refreshments – options are shown in the 'Food and Drink' box at the end of each tour.

For our pick of the tours by theme, consult Recommended Routes for… (see pages 6–7).

INTRODUCTION

The routes are set in context by this introductory section, giving an overview of the destination to set the scene, plus background information on food and drink, shopping and more, while a succinct history timeline highlights the key events over the centuries.

DIRECTORY

Also supporting the routes is a Directory chapter, with a clearly organised A–Z of practical information, our pick of where to stay while you are there and select restaurant listings; these eateries complement the more low-key cafés and restaurants that feature within the routes and are intended to offer a wider choice for evening dining. Also included here are some nightlife listings and our recommendations for books and films about the destination.

ABOUT THE AUTHORS

Patrick Kinsella is a freelance journalist and editor who has the outrageously good fortune to be a dual citizen of Australia and the UK, enabling him to enjoy the delights of both and experience their vastly contrasting wonders with new eyes each time he swaps hemispheres. Researching this book before he knew he'd be writing it, he spent most of the last decade and a half living in Australia, after arriving in Sydney just in time to see in the Millennium. Since then he's seen the country's de facto capital from every conceivable angle – from the top of the Harbour Bridge to beneath the waves of the Northern Beaches. Wherever else he may wander, a little part of his brain is always sipping a schooner in the Lord Nelson Brewery Hotel in the Rocks.

This book builds on content written by Ute Junker, a Sydney native and travel writer.

CONTACT THE EDITORS

We hope you find this Explore Guide useful, interesting and a pleasure to read. If you have any questions or feedback on the text, pictures or maps, please do let us know. If you have noticed any errors or outdated facts, or have suggestions for places to include on the routes, we would be delighted to hear from you. Please drop us an email at hello@insightguides.com. Thanks!

CREDITS

Explore Sydney
Editor: Sarah Clark
Author: Patrick Kinsella
Head of Production: Rebeka Davies
Pictures: Tom Smyth
Cartography: original cartography Phoenix Mapping Ltd, updated by Carte
Photo credits: Alamy 70, 77, 136, 137; Amora Hotel 98; Axiom 63, 64, 65; Botanic Gardens Trust 41, 93; Four Seasons 96ML, 99; Getty Images 4/5T, 7MR, 28/29T, 48, 50, 63L, 67L, 76, 82, 92, 96/97T, 118, 119, 121; Glyn Genin/Apa Publications 4ML, 4MC, 4MR, 4MC, 6TL, 6MC, 6ML, 6BC, 7MR, 12B, 12/13, 14, 16, 17, 18, 19L, 20, 21L, 20/21, 23, 28MC, 28ML, 28MR, 30, 31L, 30/31, 33, 34, 35, 36, 37L, 36/37, 38, 39, 40, 42, 43, 45L, 51, 52, 54, 56, 57L, 56/57, 59, 60, 61L, 60/61, 66, 67, 69L, 72, 74/75, 80, 90T, 94, 96MC, 110, 111L, 110/111, 112, 113, 114, 116, 117, 122, 126, 127, 128, 129, 130, 131, 132; Guillaume at Bennelong 8MC; Heidrun Lohr 22; Hilton Hotels 100; iStock 4ML, 8ML, 8MC, 8ML, 10/11, 13L, 15, 17L, 19, 24, 25L, 28MR, 28MC, 35L, 44, 45, 46, 47L, 46/47, 55, 68, 73, 78/79, 86, 87L, 86/87, 88, 89, 91, 95L, 123, 124/125, 134/135; Leonardo 102; Longrain 96MR, 96MC, 96ML, 115; Mary Evans Picture Library 27; Neal Jennings 49; Pictures Colour Library 71; Scala 26; Shangri-La Hotels & Resorts 101; Shangri-La Hotels 108; Shutterstock 6/7M, 53, 133; TFE Hotels 96MR, 104, 105, 106, 107; The Governors Table 109; Tourism Australia 1, 8/9T, 28ML, 32, 74, 75L; Tourism New South Wales 4MR, 6/7T, 8MR, 8MR, 12T, 25, 62, 69, 81, 83, 84, 85, 90B, 95; Vulcan Hotel 103
Cover credits: Getty (main) Shutterstock (BL)

Printed by CTPS – China

DISTRIBUTION

Worldwide
APA Publications (Singapore) Pte
7030 Ang Mo Kio Ave 5, 08-65
Northstar @ AMK, Singapore 569880
Email: apasin@singnet.com.sg
UK and Ireland
Dorling Kindersley Ltd (a Penguin Company)
80 Strand, London, WC2R 0RL, UK
Email: sales@uk.dk.com
US
Ingram Publisher Services
One Ingram Blvd, PO Box 3006, La Vergne, TN 37086-1986
Email: ips@ingramcontent.com
Australia and New Zealand
Woodslane
10 Apollo St, Warriewood NSW 2102, Australia
Email: info@woodslane.com.au

INDEX

MAP LEGEND

- ● Start of tour
- → Tour & route direction
- ❶ Recommended sight
- ❷ Recommended restaurant/café
- ★ Place of interest
- ❶ Tourist information
- ✉ Main post office
- ⚱ Statue/monument
- ⋔ Museum/gallery
- 📖 Library
- Theatre
- ☀ Viewpoint

- Monorail
- Light Rail
- 🚈 CityRail station
- Railway
- Motorway
- Ferry route
- 🚌 Main bus station
- 🚠 Cable car
- ✈ Airport
- Lighthouse
- Beach
- Cave
- ▲ Summit
- Ancient Site

- Cathedral/church
- † Monastery
- National boundary
- County boundary
- Park
- Important building
- Hotel
- Transport hub
- Shopping /market
- Pedestrian area
- Urban area
- Non-urban area
- Cemetery
- National park

INSIGHTGUIDES.COM

The Insight Guides website offers a unique way to plan and book tailor-made trips online. Be inspired by our curated destination content, read our daily travel blog and build your own dream trip from our range of customisable experiences, created by our local experts.

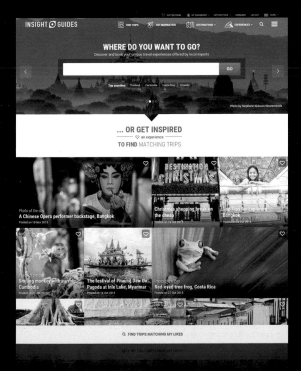

Visit our homepage and be inspired by our selection of fascinating travel stories, stunning photography and lively blogs.

Choose your dream trip from our carefully selected range of destinations, devised by trusted local experts.

Customise your perfect trip – choose your hotel, add experiences and excursions – and book securely online.

TRAVEL MADE EASY. ASK LOCAL EXPERTS.